REV. CHAS. H. SPURGEON.

CHRIST OUR ALL

CHARLES SPURGEON

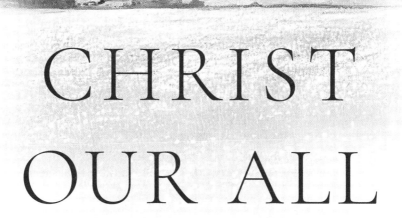

CHRIST
OUR ALL

Poems for the Christian Pilgrim

Compiled by Geoffrey Chang

ACADEMIC
BRENTWOOD, TENNESSEE

To my dear wife,

A companion in married love,

Fellow pilgrim to the world above.

CONTENTS

CONTENTS

Contents

The Published Poems & Hymns of C. H. Spurgeon

CONTENTS

ABBREVIATIONS

Autobiography   *C. H. Spurgeon's Autobiography: Compiled from His Diary, Letters, and Records, by His Wife, and His Private Secretary.* Vols. 1–4. London: Passmore & Alabaster, 1897–1900.

MTP   *The Metropolitan Tabernacle Pulpit: Sermons Preached and Revised by C. H. Spurgeon.* Vols. 7–63. London: Passmore & Alabaster, 1897–1900.

NPSP   *The New Park Street Pulpit: Containing Sermons Preached and Revised by the Rev. C. H. Spurgeon, Minister of the Chapel.* Vols. 1–6. Pasadena, TX: Pilgrim, 1975–91.

OOH   *Our Own Hymn-Book: A Collection of Psalms and Hymns for Public, Social, and Private Worship.* London: Passmore & Alabaster, 1869.

SOOH   *Supplement to Our Own Hymn-Book: A Collection of Psalms and Hymns for Public, Social, and Private Worship.* London: Passmore & Alabaster, 1898.

S&T   *The Sword and the Trowel; A Record of Combat with Sin & Labour for the Lord.* 37 vols. London: Passmore & Alabaster, 1865–1902.

TD   *The Treasury of David: Containing an Original Exposition of the Book of Psalms; a Collection of Illustrative Extracts from the Whole Range of Literature; a Series of Homiletical Hints upon Almost Every Verse; and Lists of Writers upon Each Psalm.* 7 vols. London: Passmore & Alabaster, 1869–85.

FOREWORD

I am a pilgrim in the world, but at home in my God. In Earth I
wander, but in God I dwell in a quiet habitation.
—Charles Spurgeon, *Morning by Morning,*
Or, Daily Readings for the Family or the Closet (1858)

Books of poetry fail to fill the shelves of Christian households today. Perhaps there may be a beloved hymnal, an edition of the Psalter, or a volume of Herbert or Cowper, but rarely does a home library brave further beyond. Yet, church history's treasure chest of devotional poetry contains many riches that would profit believers today. The book you hold in your hand is such a treasure.

With this collection of poems and hymns, Dr. Geoff Chang has retrieved an entire trove of poems ablaze with truth and teeming with bright affection for God, all flowing from the pen of Charles Haddon Spurgeon. His public ministry aptly earned him the title "Prince of Preachers." Yet his way with words was not limited to the pulpit. In the "quiet habitation" of his private life, his prayers poured forth in poetry. For years I have sat in the back of the class in the "School of Spurgeon" and have been indelibly influenced by his love for the truth and how to communicate it. The sermons of Spurgeon were delivered in powerful prose that also moved with the pulse of poetry and hymnody. The poems of Spurgeon are prayers set to rhythm, piety fixed to rhyme. Working through them is like hearing the heartbeat of devotion behind the pastor with such a prominent preaching ministry.

It is right that this volume has been titled *Christ Our All: Poems for the Christian Pilgrim*. There is a sense of journey to them and dependently walking with God to the Celestial City. There is present in these words a thick sense of the way Spurgeon knew communion with Christ—communion experienced through hearing his Savior speak through his Word and then responding in prayer. My prayer for you, dear fellow pilgrim, is that these poems might also lift your eyes to behold the beauty and glory of Christ.

—Matthew Boswell
hymn writer, pastor, The Trails Church, Celina, Texas,
November 2022

INTRODUCTION

Charles Haddon Spurgeon (1834–92) was, perhaps, the greatest preacher of the nineteenth century. Throughout his forty-year preaching ministry, he regularly preached four times a week (and sometimes as many as thirteen) to packed audiences of thousands. Millions of copies of these sermons were published and sold throughout the world, being translated into nearly forty languages, and they continue to be read today. But Spurgeon did not merely occupy a preaching station; he was a pastor. Beginning in London at age nineteen, Spurgeon pastored what would become the Metropolitan Tabernacle. Though there were only a few dozen in attendance when he first arrived, its membership would grow to over 5,000 members by the end of his ministry, becoming the world's largest evangelical church in his day. Spurgeon was also a philanthropist. With such a large church, Spurgeon was concerned that it engage the poor in London with the gospel. Out of the Tabernacle came dozens of evangelistic and charitable institutions, including two orphanages that Spurgeon founded and oversaw. On top of all that, Spurgeon was also a college president. Through the Pastors' College, he trained and sent out more than 900 men into church pastorates and the mission field.

Spurgeon, the preacher, pastor, philanthropist, college president. But according to his friends, there is, perhaps, another "p" that should be added to his accomplishments: Spurgeon, the poet. In compiling her husband's

Autobiography, Susannah Spurgeon wrote, "If there had been sufficient space available, an interesting chapter might have been compiled concerning 'Mr. Spurgeon as a Poet and Hymn-writer.'"[1] Eric Hayden, one of Spurgeon's successors at the Tabernacle, considered Spurgeon's hymn-writing "a much-neglected aspect of Spurgeon's genius."[2] Now, to be fair, given how influential his preaching and other ministries were, it would be a stretch to say that his poetry had a similar impact. At the same time, there is no question that Spurgeon loved poetry, that poetry permeated his ministry, and that he, in fact, contributed to Christian hymnody.

Spurgeon's Love of Poetry

Spurgeon's love of poetry can be seen today in the Spurgeon Library in Kansas City, Missouri. In his collection, we find over 200 books of poetry and hymnody, occupying several cabinets. So much of Spurgeon's life and ministry can be traced through these books.

Nearly one-third of these volumes are hymnbooks for Christian worship, including Horatius Bonar's *Hymns of Faith and Hope*; Anne Steele's *Hymns, Psalms, and Poems*; Isaac Watts's *Hymns and Spiritual Songs*, and many others. Spurgeon's love of hymns began at a young age. Once, during a summer holiday, his grandmother offered him a penny for each Watts hymn he memorized. With his gifted mind, young Spurgeon memorized so many that his grandmother soon had to change her offer or risk financial ruin! The money earned was eventually spent, but his love of hymns remained with him for the rest of his life, becoming a part of his theological vocabulary. "No matter on what topic I am preaching," he wrote, "I can

---

[1] *Autobiography* 4:313.

[2] Eric W. Hayden, *Highlights in the Life of Charles Haddon Spurgeon* (Pasadena, TX: Pilgrim Publications, 1990), 101. He suggests, "Some aspiring student seeking a doctoral thesis subject might well study the hymns and poems of the Prince of Preachers."

even now, in the middle of any sermon, quote some verse of a hymn in harmony with the subject."[3] As Spurgeon grew in his knowledge of hymns, his sermons would come to include not only Watts, but Toplady, Cowper, Wesley, and many other great hymn-writers of the Christian faith.

As the pastor of a church, Spurgeon sought to pass on his love of hymns to his congregants. In addition to preaching, he planned the liturgy for the gatherings of the church, including the selection of hymns. When he first arrived, there were two hymnbooks in the pews, one by Watts and the other by John Rippon. But watching people fumble with multiple books convinced Spurgeon that something had to change. So, in 1866, he compiled and published *Our Own Hymn-Book*, containing 1,130 psalms and hymns. As reflected in the title, Spurgeon's concern was the church. This was not Spurgeon's hymnbook; this was the church's hymnbook. One of his top priorities was to pull together psalms and hymns that reflected the church's doctrinal convictions. After all, Spurgeon understood that a church's hymnbook was often the only book of theology most church members would ever read.

But even while *Our Own Hymn-Book* reflected Spurgeon's Reformed and Baptist traditions, he also sought to introduce a wide variety of traditions, pulling together hymns from all of church history. He wrote:

> The area of our researches has been as wide as the bounds of existing religious literature, American and British, Protestant and Romish; ancient and modern. Whatever may be thought of our taste we have used it without prejudice; and a good hymn has not been rejected because of the character of its author, or the heresies of the church in whose hymnal it first occurred; so long as the language and the spirit commended the hymn to our heart we included it, and believe that we have enriched our collection thereby.[4]

---

[3] *Autobiography* 1:43–44.
[4] *OOH*, vi–vii.

Thus, we see in Spurgeon's collection of hymnbooks a wide variety of hymn writers: Scottish Presbyterians, English Baptists and Methodists, German Lutherans, Anglicans, medieval Catholics, and other nationalities and church traditions, ranging from the nineteenth century all the way back to the medieval and early church. From all these psalms and hymns, Spurgeon sought to bring out the ones that best reflected the historic faith of the apostles and the church's doctrinal convictions. In his day, *Our Own Hymn-Book* was recognized as an achievement in Christian hymnody.[5]

But Spurgeon's love of poetry extended beyond hymns. His library reveals that Spurgeon enjoyed just about every kind of poetry: ancient poetry, poems about nature, love poems, children's rhymes, and many others. Most of all, however, Spurgeon loved poems about God and the Christian life. Preaching in 1855, Spurgeon declared, "Much as I respect the genius of Pope, or Dryden, or Burns, give me the simple lines of Cowper, that God has owned in bringing souls to Him."[6] William Cowper was indeed one of Spurgeon's favorite poets. He usually included Cowper's famous hymn whenever he signed autograph albums, "E'er since by faith I saw the stream . . ."[7] Fittingly, these lines are etched on his tombstone.

Another poet he loved was John Bunyan. Throughout his life, he read, "at least a hundred times," *The Pilgrim's Progress*, "that sweetest of all prose poems," which shaped his vision for the Christian life.[8] What he loved most

---

[5] For an appreciative nineteenth-century analysis of Spurgeon's contribution to Christian hymnody, see Josiah Miller, *Singers and Songs of the Church: Being Biographical Sketches of the Hymn-Writers in All the Principal Collections: with Notes on their Psalms and Hymns* (London: Longmans, Green, 1869), 580–81.

[6] *NPSP* 1:344.

[7] Hayden, *Highlights,* 101.

[8] *MTP* 45:495.

about it was simply how much Bible was in it.[9] Bunyan brought together Spurgeon's love of Scripture with his love of poetry.

Yet another of his favorite poets was George Herbert. Herbert was a source of refreshment for Spurgeon, especially after a long day of ministry.[10] His wife, Susannah, recounted:

> It is the Sabbath, and the day's work is done. The dear preacher has had a light repast, and now rests in his easy chair by a bright fire, while, on a low cushion at his feet, sits his wife, eager to minister in some way to her beloved's comfort. "Shall I read to you to-night, dear?" she says; for the excitement and labor of the Sabbath services sorely try him, and his mind needs some calm and soothing influence to set it at rest. "Will you have a page or two of good George Herbert?" "Yes, that will be very refreshing, wifey; I shall like that." So the book is procured, and he chooses a portion which I read slowly and with many pauses, that he may interpret to me the sweet mysteries hidden within the gracious words. Perhaps his enjoyment of the book is all the greater that he has thus to explain and open out to me the precious truths enwrapped in Herbert's quaint verse; —anyhow, the time is delightfully spent. I read on and on for an

---

[9] "Next to the Bible, the book I value most is John Bunyan's 'Pilgrim's Progress.' I believe I have read it through at least a hundred times. It is a volume of which I never seem to tire; and the secret of its freshness is that it is so largely compiled from the Scriptures. It is really Biblical teaching put into the form of a simple yet very striking allegory." C. H. Spurgeon, *Pictures from Pilgrim's Progress: A Commentary on Portions of John Bunyan's Immortal Allegory with Prefatory Notes by Thomas Spurgeon* (Pasadena, TX: Pilgrim Publications, 1992), 11.

[10] "Frequently, when I return home from chapel on the Sabbath evening, I get down George Herbert's book of songs; and when I see how much he loved the Lord, it seems to me as if he had struck upon his harp the very notes that he had heard in Paradise, and sung them all again." *MTP* 46:106.

hour or more, till the peace of Heaven flows into our souls, and
the tired servant of the King of kings loses his sense of fatigue, and
rejoices after his toil.[11]

For Spurgeon, poetry was about more than just entertainment. It gave him
the perspective of a Christian pilgrim. It provided spiritual nourishment for
his tired soul. And it strengthened him with a renewed joy in God for the
week ahead.

But not all poetry was so edifying. As the editor of a monthly magazine,
The Sword and the Trowel, Spurgeon was often sent new works of poetry
for review. Some of these poems were featured among his book notices,
and Spurgeon sought to commend edifying works of poetry to his readers.
On Adam Todd's *Poems, Lectures, and Miscellanies*, Spurgeon commented,
"Mr. Todd writes in a very capital style, with much poetic feeling. His work
is not quite in our line of things, nor could we endorse all he says, but we
doubt not that many will while away an hour pleasantly with his poems
and lectures."[12] However, such (barely) positive reviews were rare compared
to how many volumes he rejected. In 1884, "the Long-Suffering Editor of
'*The Sword and the Trowel*'" published an article titled "Where Not to Send
Poems or Blank Verse."[13] There, Spurgeon begged the aspiring poet:

> Milton and Thomson, Young and Cowper, we can all rejoice in;
> but your ordinary imitator of these sweet singers is blank as blank-
> ness itself. When the dear man feels that he must cover reams of
> paper with his effervescences, we have not the remotest objection
> to his doing so: it may be good for the paper-trade and good for
> himself; BUT, with the utmost vehemence of our outraged nature,
> we entreat him not to send his manuscripts to us, that we may pass

---

[11] *Autobiography* 2:185–86.
[12] *S&T* 1877:391.
[13] *S&T* 1884:351.

our opinion upon them, and introduce them to a publisher. This is one of our afflictions, and by no means a light one. The quantity of time it takes to answer poets we dare not attempt to calculate. Moreover, there is the solemn responsibility of having such jewels to take care of. We do not feel worthy to have the charge of such priceless treasures. Burglars might run off with them, rats might eat them, our Mary might either sell them to the waste-paper man, or they might even drop into

THE RECEPTACLE BELOW.

Clearly, Spurgeon's poetry collection would've been much larger had all the books and manuscripts of poetry he received been fireproof!

While Spurgeon's rejection of those volumes was done in good humor, there was one work of poetry that raised more serious concerns. In 1855, Thomas T. Lynch published *The Rivulet: A Contribution to Sacred Song*. *The Rivulet* was highly reviewed in several evangelical newspapers by numerous ministers, and soon, some congregations began to use it in their corporate worship. But in the following year, some began to raise serious charges against the book. While the hymns contained references to God and to his beauty in nature, critics charged it as "seriously defective with regard to the essentials of vital Christianity," particularly in doctrines like the person of

Christ, the atonement, and total depravity.[14] These charges sparked a series of articles throughout the winter and spring of 1856 defending and criticizing *The Rivulet*. Finally, in May 1856, the twenty-one-year-old Spurgeon weighed in.

Writing his editorial in *The Christian Cabinet*, Spurgeon had no objections to *The Rivulet* as a work of poetry. He commented, "When reading these hymns, simply as literary compositions, I found them far from despicable. There is true poetry in some of them, of a very delicate and refined order. Every now and then, the voices of the flowers or of the rain-drops are clear and soft, and perpetually the thinkings of the poet wake an echo in the soul."[15]

Despite these restrained compliments, Spurgeon made it clear that it was far from perfect. He found some of the lines "unintelligible," with no clear connection to one another. "There is much mist, and a large proportion of fog." Overall, he judged that "there is nothing very wonderful in the book."[16] In these comments, we get a preview of the long-suffering editor of *The Sword and the Trowel*!

But Lynch did not advertise this book as merely a book of poems. Rather, in his introduction, he claims that it is a book of hymns "suitable for the chamber or the church," to be "said or sung" as worship to God. It was on this point that Spurgeon stated his main objection to *The Rivulet*: these hymns were so lacking in clear theological content that they were unsuitable for the worship of the church. "There is so little of the doctrinal element in them that I am at a loss to judge; and that little is so indefinite that, apart from the author's antecedents, one could scarcely guess his doctrinal views at all. Certainly, some verses are bad, — bad in the most

---

[14] *Autobiography* 2:260.
[15] *Autobiography* 2:264.
[16] *Autobiography* 2:264.

unmitigated sense of that word; but others of them, like noses of wax, will fit more than one face."[17]

Being so vague theologically, Spurgeon believed they could be sung by any worshipper of nature. "O ye Delawares, Mohawks, Choctaws, Chickasaws, Blackfeet, Pawnees, Shawnees, and Cherokees, here is your primitive faith most sweetly rehearsed, — not in your own wild notes, but in the white man's language."[18] In other words, for a hymn to be suitable for the singing of the church, it must be distinctly Christian in its theology. If a hymn can be gladly sung by pantheists, or Muslims, or Jews, or Unitarians, or the adherents of any other religion, then it is not suitable for the church's worship. Christian hymns must declare boldly the sinful condition of man. They must proclaim Jesus, the Savior of the world. And they must glorify God, as he has revealed himself in the Scriptures. Only such hymns will "cheer us on our dying bed" and "nerve us with faith for a living conflict."[19]

The controversy over *The Rivulet* would soon pass. But Spurgeon saw signs of something far more ominous. With so many pastors showing little discernment and so many churches adopting *The Rivulet* as their hymn-book, Spurgeon could see a battle over theological orthodoxy brewing on the horizon. "This controversy," he said, "is but one volcano indicative of seas of latent fire in the bosom of our churches. It will, in a few more years, be hard to prove the orthodoxy of our churches if matters be not changed. It has manifested what existed already; it has dragged to light evils which were before unseen."[20] Written in 1856, these words would prove to be prophetic, as Spurgeon would spend the last years of his life fighting for theological orthodoxy in his own denomination.

---

[17] *Autobiography* 2:265.
[18] *Autobiography* 2:266.
[19] *Autobiography* 2:267.
[20] *Autobiography* 2:267.

Spurgeon's Poems

In addition to loving poetry, Spurgeon tried his hand at writing poems. The second part of this volume contains forty-three poems written by Spurgeon that were published during his life or soon afterward. Several of the poems, like "The Dropping Well of Knaresborough" or "Popery," were published in *The Sword and the Trowel* for the edification of his readers. Four were written when Spurgeon was a teenager, pastoring at Waterbeach. Three are personal poems: one a love poem to his wife; another a tribute to his friend and secretary, Joseph Harrald; and a third a note of gratitude for care and hospitality received at the Hotel des Anglais. The majority of Spurgeon's published poetry (twenty-nine poems, to be exact) were psalms and hymns published in *Our Own Hymn-Book* and its supplement.

A few observations about these published poems: Spurgeon spent most of his creativity on content rather than structure or form. His poetry typically follows common rhyme schemes and meters, likely influenced by his love of English hymns. The characteristics that stand out are the energy of his imagery and the bold doctrinal convictions expressed in his verses. Spurgeon's poems have a lively and deeply theological quality. For example, his poem "Immanuel" describes the cry of the soul amid the storms of life:

> When storms of sorrow toss my soul,
> When waves of care around me roll,
> When comforts sink, when joys shall flee,
> When hopeless gulfs shall gape for me,
> One word the tempest's rage shall quell,
> That word, Thy name, Immanuel!

In "Popery," in response to growing influence of Roman Catholicism in his day, Spurgeon does not pull any punches when declaring his Protestant convictions:

No priestly witchcraft can absolve
A sin however small,
But to the Saviour we must go,
His blood can cleanse from all.

In other words, Spurgeon's poems reflect his own active and bold faith. This is how he lived and preached, and this is what was expressed in his poetry.

One may also observe that many of Spurgeon's published poems reveal a life rooted in the church and his role as a pastor. *Our Own Hymn-Book* included several original compositions by Spurgeon, but he did not write these hymns spontaneously. For the versified psalms, he composed them because "he could find no version at all fitted for singing, and was therefore driven to turn them into verse himself."[21] As someone committed to singing through the Psalter, Spurgeon wanted to make sure that there was a singable hymn for every psalm, even if that meant composing some himself. Similarly, he found a lack of hymns that addressed the life of the church. With so many churches in his day looking for pastors, he composed "Lord, Thy Church, without a Pastor," a hymn to be sung by the congregation as a prayer for God's provision of a faithful shepherd. Similarly, "Risen Lord, Thou Hast Received" recognizes new elders and deacons in the church, praying for God's blessing on their ministry. Another hymn, "Amidst Us Our Beloved Stands," celebrates Christ's spiritual presence in the Lord's Supper. What these psalms and hymns reveal is that so many of Spurgeon's original compositions were based on the needs and the life of the church. In other words, his published poems correspond to his public ministry as a pastor.

It must also be said that in addition to these forty-three poems, there are countless verses and rhymes found in Spurgeon's sermons that have no attribution and appear to be original to him. A truly complete publication

---

[21] *OOH*, x.

of Spurgeon's poetry would have to include these lines, but such a massive task is beyond the scope of this volume.

While he was not afraid to publish his own poetry, Spurgeon hoped for a measure of charity from his readers when evaluating them. In his introduction to *Our Own Hymn-book*, Spurgeon notes, "As these original compositions are but few, it is hoped that they will not prejudice the ordinary reader against the rest of the collection, and possibly one or two of them may gratify the generous judgment of our friends."[22] Even while he tried his hand at poetry, Spurgeon knew that his calling and giftedness were primarily as a pastor and preacher, not a poet or a hymn-writer.

The Private Poems

The most unique contribution of this volume, however, is the first section, containing Spurgeon's unpublished, or private, poems. Residing in the Spurgeon Library is a notebook containing 186 handwritten poems. This notebook was part of the original collection, which was purchased by the Missouri Baptists in 1906 and came to Midwestern Seminary in 2006.[23] On the back cover of the notebook is a bookplate with Charles Jr. and Thomas Spurgeon's signatures, attesting that this book belonged to their father's library.[24] There is no title page, but on the spine are two simple words:

Poems

Spurgeon

---

[22] *OOH*, x.

[23] For a history of Spurgeon's library before its acquisition by Midwestern Baptist Theological Seminary, see Adrian Lamkin, "The Spurgeon Library of William Jewell College: A Hidden Treasure among Baptists in America," *Baptist History and Heritage* 19, no. 4 (October 1984): 39–44.

[24] Nearly all the books in the Spurgeon Library contain a similar bookplate.

It would seem obvious that these poems were written by Charles Haddon Spurgeon, but there are a few complicating factors. First, there is no stated author within the notebook, either on a title page or for any individual poem, with one exception. In the upper-right corner of poem 69, "Bethesda's Pool," is written "C. H. Spurgeon Aug / 62." Why is there an attribution for only one poem? What does that mean about the rest of them? Second, and perhaps more significantly, the handwriting in the book does not match Spurgeon's handwriting.[25] If this is not Spurgeon's writing, then can we be sure these are his poems?

Despite these complications, I am convinced that these poems were originally written by Spurgeon, for the following reasons:

1. Spurgeon's love of poetry. As we've already seen, Spurgeon loved poetry and wrote his own poems as part of his public ministry. So, it should not surprise us that he would have a collection of unpublished poems in his possession. If this had been a notebook of drawings or music, it would be harder to believe that they came from Spurgeon. But as one who loved poetry, it is not surprising that Spurgeon would have poems that were never published.

2. Theological themes. Spurgeon's love of poetry intersected with his faith, and we see this same intersection in these poems. If the content of these poems was primarily about nature or travel, then perhaps they might suggest another author. But nearly all these poems are religious in content, written as private prayers or devotional exercises, expressing his sorrows, hopes, and love for God.

---

[25] Regarding the handwriting of these poems, Veeneenea Erika Smith writes, "Handwriting analysts determined that the handwriting is not Spurgeon's; however it is important to remember that he had secretaries and a wife who could have gathered and copied the work either before or after his death." Smith, "Dinna Forget Spurgeon: A Literary Biography" (PhD diss., Case Western Reserve University, 2006), 272.

Furthermore, when we examine the theological content of these poems, they clearly align with Spurgeon's teaching. These poems reflect theological themes of God, Christ, salvation, sanctification, the church, the sacraments, final judgment, and much more—themes that reflect Spurgeon's Reformed theological tradition and are in line with much of his sermons and writings elsewhere.

3. Biographical details. There are biographical details in the poems that align with what we know about Spurgeon's life and ministry. I will highlight three. Poem 89, "Metropolitan Tabernacle Dedicated," points to the spring of 1861, when multiple services were held to dedicate the magnificent new building. In this poem, Spurgeon prays for God's blessing:

> This house is thine; 'tis raised for thee
> And dedicated to thy praise.
> Let holiness its portals be,
> And in this house bestow thy grace.[26]

Poem 162, "Sickness," is also particularly biographical. As one who wrestled with gout, rheumatism, kidney disease, and all kinds of other physical ailments, Spurgeon knew well the trials of sickness. In this poem, the poet, like Job, laments his trial and offers no answers for his questions:

> Why send the many ills to swell,
> Through which poor mortals tread?
> Are there not woes enough to tell
> To lay us with the dead?[27]

---

[26] *Poems*, 89.
[27] *Poems*, 162.

Finally, poem 59, "Come Ye Out from Among Them," expresses the importance of separation of Christians from the world:

> Quite separate, ye chosen of the Lord,
> Ye stand amid a host of foes.
> "Come from among them," is his word,
> "In me ye find your sure repose."[28]

Such a poem could have been written by Spurgeon during the 1864 Baptismal Regeneration controversy, when he called evangelicals to leave the Church of England for her tolerance of the growing Oxford movement. Or it could have been written in the late 1880s, during the Downgrade Controversy, when Spurgeon resigned from the Baptist Union over her compromise with theological liberalism.[29] Many more biographical connections could be made with these poems, but these three provide a notable sampling.

4. Handwriting on the spine. While the handwriting in the notebook does not match Spurgeon's, the handwriting on the spine is different. When comparing Spurgeon's print handwriting with the handwriting on the spine, there appears to be a notable similarity.[30] It's not a perfect match, but given that he was writing in print letters, on a narrow, curved spine, some variation is to be

---

[28] *Poems*, 59.

[29] For an analysis of Spurgeon's involvement in these controversies and others, see Iain Murray, *The Forgotten Spurgeon* (Edinburgh: Banner of Truth Trust, 2002).

[30] For an example of Spurgeon's print handwriting, see C. H. Spurgeon, *The Letters of Charles Haddon Spurgeon: Collected and Collated by His Son Charles Spurgeon* (New York: Marshall Brothers, 1923), 4. Samples of Spurgeon's print handwriting can also be found on some of his sermon notes. See *Sermon Notes Display*, Spurgeon Library Archive.

expected. There are enough similarities to indicate that this notebook belonged to Spurgeon.

Given his love of poetry, the biographical and theological connections, the bookplate, the clear attribution of poem 69, and the corresponding handwriting on the spine, I'm convinced that these poems were all originally written by Spurgeon.

If these poems were originally written by Spurgeon, how did this volume of poems come to be? There are a few clues about the notebook's composition. First, it appears that the poems were written throughout Spurgeon's life. There are two poems that seem to indicate this: poem 69, "Bethesda's Pool," contains the date August 1862, and poem 89, "Metropolitan Tabernacle Dedicated," points us to the spring of 1861, when public services began at the newly constructed building. The numbering of these two poems reveals that these poems are not in chronological order. These two dates also indicate that many, if not all, of these poems were composed during his ministry in London, after his arrival in the spring of 1854. Other biographical details in the poems (like his illness, his heart for the lost, or his exhaustion from ministry) would be characteristic of much of his life, so it's hard to pinpoint a specific period.

Second, the handwriting, the quality of the ink, and the style and formatting of the poems are consistent throughout the notebook, indicating that the poems were copied all around the same time, perhaps even in one sitting. This would explain the attribution for poem 69. Spurgeon wrote the date and attribution on the original, perhaps intending it for publication, and the copier simply copied it over to the notebook.[31]

My theory, then, is that these poems were composed throughout his life in multiple notebooks and pieces of papers. But at some point, perhaps

---

[31] "If they are not in Spurgeon's hand, the scribe was careful to record every marking from the original page even dating one of the poems 'Aug' 69' underneath the words 'C. H. Spurgeon.'" Smith, "Dinna Forget the Spurgeon," 272.

near his death, Spurgeon expressed his intention for them to be collected, preparing this notebook for that purpose, which explains the handwriting on the spine. Then, perhaps after his death, these poems were copied into the notebook by one of his associates.

Unfortunately, the identity of the copier remains a mystery. We know that Susannah and Harrald, his secretary, worked through many of Spurgeon's papers after his death to prepare for the publication of his four-volume *Autobiography*. Harrald knew of Spurgeon's love of poetry, so he might have played a part in bringing the poems together.[32] But in comparing existing handwriting samples, I've been able to rule out Susannah and Harrald, along with other, more obvious options—Charles Spurgeon Jr., Thomas Spurgeon, and Archibald Brown. Other options remain—G. H. Pike, Robert Shindler, Joseph Passmore, and other close associates.[33] Perhaps a future scholar will be able to discover more clues as to the origins of this notebook.

In transcribing these poems, I have tried to stick as closely as possible to the original manuscript. The original spelling has been mostly retained, except in cases of misspellings or archaic spellings. I have also added punctuation and spacing between verses for clarity and readability. The poem titles come from Spurgeon. Several of them are simply entitled "Prayer." For these, I've added the first line to the title to help distinguish those poems. For poems with identical titles, I've added a parenthetical Roman numeral to distinguish them.

As noted earlier, Spurgeon's poetry is intimately tied with his love of Scripture. Because this volume is meant to be read devotionally, I have also added a related biblical text for each poem. Spurgeon undoubtedly would affirm that these poems have devotional value only insofar as they accurately

---

[32] *Autobiography* 4:223–24.

[33] Susannah lists the associates that regularly accompanied Spurgeon to southern France during his travels there to recover his health. See *Autobiography* 4:198–200.

reflect the truths of Scripture. So even as you enjoy the poetry, take time also to reflect on God's promises *to you*. Consider your own struggles and challenges, doubts and fears. What difference would it make in your life if you held on to these truths with the same kind of faith and hope that Spurgeon had? These poems are not meant to be rushed through, but to be read slowly, thoughtfully, and prayerfully. May these poems point you not only to the truth, but also to the beauty of Christ.

With the title of this volume, *Christ Our All: Poems for the Christian Pilgrim*, I have sought to identify a unifying theme for the private poems, and perhaps even for all of Spurgeon's poetry, namely his vision of the Christian life as a pilgrimage to heaven. These poems reveal the prayers of one who knows that this world is not his home, and that he is headed to the Celestial City. Nearly every poem concludes with this theme. For example, in poem 105, "Hear Infants' Praise," Spurgeon concludes with the prayer that these children would praise God not only in this life but in eternity:

Young in the paths of sin, they stray;
O, let them fear thy law,
And after time, in endless day,
Thy wondrous grace adore.

In poem 151, "Fear Not, for I Am Thy God," Spurgeon reflects on God's enduring faithfulness through trials and concludes with this exhortation and hope:

Silence my heart, give hear my soul,
Remember still he loves.
His word, his oath, is pledg'd to call
Us up to where he lives.

Some poems are devoted entirely to this theme. For example, poem 51, "Rest," begins by recounting the sweetness of the promise of eternal rest for those "whose tot'ring weary feet / bespeak the pilgrim's early close / with life." These words could very well have been autobiographical, as Spurgeon was afflicted by gout in his feet for much of his ministry. In all his afflictions, could it be that he foresaw an early death? And yet these trials were reminders of a greater hope. "Bound to this house of clay / Waiting the summons for to rise / And dwell in joyous day." Spurgeon reflected not only on the journey, but also the destination. Like a soldier looking longingly at pictures of his family and his homeland, these poems reflect the pilgrim's longing for his heavenly home:

> Yon bright world is beaming
> With the fairest of delights.
> Pleasures ever streaming,
> My weary soul invites.[34]

By making heaven the concluding theme of so many of his poems, Spurgeon followed a rich tradition in Christian hymnody. So many of the church's favorite hymns, "A Mighty Fortress," "Come Thou Fount," "It Is Well," "Solid Rock," "How Great Thou Art," and countless others, conclude by declaring the Christian's hope of heaven and God's ultimate triumph over evil. But as much as Christians might enjoy such endings, this is not merely a matter of aesthetics. The hope of heaven is a biblical and theological conviction. By concluding with the hope of heaven, these poems follow the overarching storyline of Scripture, proclaiming our hope in the return of Christ and his eternal kingdom.

For Spurgeon the weary pilgrim, it was this perspective that he needed to keep before his eyes as he faced the trials and sorrows of life. For Spurgeon the Christian, every poem and every trial, no matter how dark, found its resolution not in this life, but in the one to come.

---

[34] Poem 57, "Yon Bright World."

Then what a joyful day t'will be
When thou shalt call me home;
Always thy glorious face to see
And never more to roam.

And through the hills in endless life
Where cherubs wing their flight,
Secure from every sin and strife,
I'll dwell within thy sight.[35]

---

[35] Poem 139, "Guidance."

The Private Poems
of C. H. Spurgeon

Prayer: Captain of Our Salvation, Prove

Captain of our salvation, prove
The greatness of thy saving love;
Teach thou this wayward heart to know
What made thee love poor sinners so.

Was it for aught that we had done
For thee, that thy great pity came?
Or that because our helpless state
Bespoke the rebel sinner[']s fate?

Was it for love we bore thy name
That made thee bear the cross and shame?
Or that because our sins were deep
That made thy loving heart to weep?

Lord, did our ruin bring thee down
And make thee leave thy royal crown?
To wander here, endure the grave
Our sinful souls to buy and save?

Did our condition grieve thy heart
And bring thee down to bear our smart?
Or did thy loving heart desire
To save us from eternal fire?

If such great love as this was thine
To us a mass of guilt and sin,
Let me adore thy sovereign grace;
Save me, and let me see thy face.

FOR FURTHER REFLECTION: 1 TIMOTHY 1:15—16

PRAYER: AWAKE! THIS MORN MY HEART WOULD RISE

Awake! This morn my heart would rise
Above this world to see thy face;
Beyond these narrow-cloudy skies
To gain from thee, supplies of grace.

Arise! O King thy people wait
To speak with thee, to feel thy love.
We come and waiting at thy gate,
Desire thy blessing from above.

Alone with thee, the world behind,
Our hearts are waiting thee to meet.
Still hoping in thy love to find
Our help while waiting at thy feet.

O can'st thou spurn us from thee[,] Lord
And disappoint each waiting soul?
Then thou must take away thy word,
Which bids us on thy name to call.

But wilt thou have us here to doubt
Thy goodness, love, forgiving heart?
Shall our petition be cast out?
Once sav'd, Lord, wilt thou from us part?

O Lord we cannot think of thee
With such hard thoughts, thy Life, thy Death
Thy rising, it was all for me
And all who love thee, Scripture saith.

FOR FURTHER REFLECTION: PSALM 63:1—4

3

THOU ART MY ALL

Dear Lord, in thee I view my all,
And lovely is thy name.
For though on earth I slip or fall,
Thy love remains the same.

Each day reminds me I am weak
To stand against my foes;
And, but that I thy help may seek,
I'd fall beneath my woes.

But thou hast said my strength shall be
According to my day.
Thy promise has been kept to me,
And still will be I pray.

For what are we if left to roam
In life's deceitful way?
Yet farther off, not nearer home,
Our feet are prone to stray.

Then never have us Lord to tread
This world without a guide.
And never let the tempter lead
Thine erring sheep aside.

"I will not leave, nor yet forsake
My people here below;
Until in glory they shall wake
And purer regions know."

FOR FURTHER REFLECTION: DEUTERONOMY 33:25—27

4

I Am Thine

My Jesus I am bound to thee
With chains that cannot break.
Thou'st promis'd I shall saved be,
And I thy word will take.

I feel within constraining love,
Which binds my heart to thine.
I hear thy word come from above
And feel that word is mine.

I know thou never can'st depart;
My name is held so dear.
'Tis this poor unbelieving heart
That gives me cause to fear.

What! Fear thee? No, thy name I'll love,
And cherish still thy word.
Thou dost the greatest sin remove
That mortals ever heard.

Then who can doubt so great a friend
Whose life our ransom paid
And still will guard us to the end
By his all pow'rful aid?

Then Jesus, take our hearts again;
They still thy sway shall own.
And when we pass from earth and pain,
We'll praise thy name alone.

FOR FURTHER REFLECTION: ISAIAH 49:15—16

5

COME DAY OF JUDGMENT

Day of judgment, speed thy wing;
Haste to close this world of woe.
Dreadful day, arrive and bring
Thy morn, and make these hearts to glow.

Nought but strife while here we stay;
Troubles, toils, we here endure.
Come to chase this scene away;
Our every trial here to cure.

Lo! Thy morn we long to see;
Thine approach our spirits crave.
Life and peace, eternity,
Come our waiting souls to save.

Nay! We wait with great desire
Till thy blessed day shall dawn.
We fear no grief, thy dread fire
Shall but make us cease to mourn.

Sinners may with anguish cry.
'Tis a dreadful day to those
Who thy gracious law defy;
Who would not with mercy close.

But thy saints, they hail the day
That shall sever them from sin.
Welcome morn, to bear away
To the realms of peace within.

FOR FURTHER REFLECTION: 1 JOHN 4:16–17

Thou Art My Delight

In thy blessed sight I'll stay,
Sit and rest my weary soul;
Never more to go away
As eternal ages roll.

In thine arms I would recline,
On thy loving bosom lean.
Make thy spirit in me shine;
From this world my soul to wean.

Dearest Jesus, make me feel
Compass'd by thy loving arms.
As before thy face I kneel,
Let me view thy lovely charms.

Dearest Lord, I long to rest
Where no earthly care can come;
By thy love forever blest
Hear thy sweetest welcome home.

O my Lord, why stay so far?
Come, I long to see thy face.
All thy people waiting are
For the beauties of thy grace.

Shall the thought distress my mind
That I soon shall pass from clay?
No, 'tis here I comfort find,
Here I enter endless day.

For further reflection: 2 Corinthians 5:6–9

7

Depart Vain World

Depart vain world, thy charms no more
Shall hold me here; I long to soar
Where music rolls in every wind,
Where peace to fill my soul I find.

Depart vain world, my aching heart
Desires me from thy ways to part.
Earth! All thy vanities I see
And long to be away from thee.

Depart vain world, I long to go
Where higher, deeper, pleasures flow;
All vanity, vexation here,
A tumult, and a life-long fear.

Depart vain world, thy sins I weep;
I wait the time when I shall sleep
Till trumpet's sound awakes the dead,
And ransom'd mortals lift their head.

Depart vain world, I am deceiv'd;
That thou hadst peace I once believed.
Betray'd I am, I now have found
Thy pleasures are but empty sound.

Depart vain world, where nought but strife
Exists, for what? This mortal life
Adieu, I leave thy land of tears
And soar away beyond thy fears.

For further reflection: Ecclesiastes 5:13–17

29

8

GOD'S GREATNESS

O Thou, the infinitely great,
Past mortals' highest thought to know,
In grand abodes, in pomp and state,
Thine hidden glories thou dost shew.

Thy greatness none on earth can see;
Creation came with but thy word.
Our minds so small; can only be
Able to grasp what they have heard.

But far beyond this scene of time,
No eye can thy bright glories scan;
Where thou in majesty dost shine,
The God that died for mortal man.

Earth at thy word sprang into life;
Heav'n with its glories heard thee call.
Confusion ceas'd at once from strife;
The elements began to fall.

Yea, at thy bidding worlds appear'd;
Space and its limits heard thy voice.
And all creation as it fear'd,
At once thy will became its choice.

Earth! Raise thy highest praises now;
Roll all ye worlds before his face.
People of every nation bow,
Adore his pow'r, extol his grace.

FOR FURTHER REFLECTION: JOHN 1:1–5

To Thee I Come

To thee I come, my Jesus Lord,
To hear from thee thy blessed word.
I feel thy love, and truth, and grace
And long to see thee face to face.

To thee I come, O let me see
The blessings thou hast brought for me,
When from this world my soul shall fly,
When death shall come and I shall die.

To thee I come, my only Friend
That will not leave me till life's end;
Whose watchful eye discerns my foes
And all their doings overthrows.

To thee I come, thou art my life,
My help in every mortal strife,
My victory, my reward above;
O leave me not, thou art my love.

To thee I come, my falt'ring breath
Whispers the near approach of death.
Thine hand I seek, to lead me through,
Till passing death, thy face I view.

To thee I come, Lord take me in;
By thee I've fought and conquer'd sin.
The prize I see, I near my home;
My Jesus Lord, to thee I come.

For further reflection: Matthew 11:28–30

ETERNITY

Eternity, thou art beyond my thought.
Minds are too small thy door alone to see.
By thee this soul of mine is taught
How vast his power, who formed thee.

O thou Jehovah, teach this heart to know;
Let some enlight'ning spark descend, I pray.
Teach me thy will; O come and shew
This darken'd soul thy truth and way.

O thou mysterious one of whom we hear,
Awe'd at thy presence, we desire to love.
Thou hidden one whom mortals fear
And long to see in realms above.

Speak! O desire of men, whisper thy name;
Bid doubts and fears on wings of light'ning fly.
Come teach this heart, kindle a flame
That lit on earth, shall burn on high.

Unseen, yet felt; unknown, yet known by all;
Within, without, at home, and yet abroad;
Dictating right within each soul;
Speak thou, whom all believe is God.

Ah! Though no voice thy will to us proclaims,
Creation speaks; earth in ten thousand forms
Demands our ear, air, sea, and flames.
We hear thy voice amid the storms.

FOR FURTHER REFLECTION: 1 TIMOTHY 6:13–16

CONSCIENCE (I)

What is this voice within my soul?
What is it makes me thus to fear?
A trembling, fearing, lest I fall,
What voice is this within I hear?

Cease, what makes thy warning cry
And makes this heart to be alarm'd?
Art thou implanted from on high
To keep my soul, by sin, when charm'd?

Where dwellest thou, thou silent friend
That constantly my soul dost guard
And night and day my steps attend?
Stay, while this heart remains so hard.

In every scene of life and death,
Remain to keep my soul awake.
Until there flies the latest breath,
Stay, with my soul, thy friendship make.

Sweet voice that bids me draw the sword,
That bids me clothe in armour bright.
Conscience, I hail thee by thy word,
I stand array'd with sin to fight.

O Thou bestower of this gift,
My highest praise to thee shall rise.
In thankfulness my heart shall lift,
On earth, and then beyond the skies.

FOR FURTHER REFLECTION: ROMANS 2:13–16

God's Faithfulness

O God, who hast thy people led
Through dangers and through storms;
In famine thou hast found them bread,
In war hast been their arms.

Mid stakes, and racks, and torments great,
Thine arm has led them through.
Leave them unto a cruel fate?
This thing thou can'st not do.

Leave them, the purchase of thy blood?
Forsake them while they stray?
Through pitfalls, lions' dens, O Lord,
Do drive this thought away.

Forsake them? This can never be!
In fires thou wilt with them be found;
Racks shall be beds of down, with thee
To heal each smarting wound.

"Forsake thee? O, I never can!
My arm remains your shield.
Trials I send your wheat to fan
That it tenfold may yield."

"Forget thee? This I cannot do.
Thou still shalt reign on high.
A mansion I prepare for you
Amid seraphic joy."

FOR FURTHER REFLECTION: PSALM 118:6—8

Be Faithful Even unto Death

Strange sounds amid a world of cares
Now fall upon my ear;
That calls me on through toils and snares
And bids me not to fear.

Be faithful even unto death,
A crown for thee is made.
'Tis thine, nor shall the slightest breath
Against thy name be said.

In every scene, he steadfast still,
Take courage and be strong.
God be thy fear, his holy will
Be all thy stay and song.

Let hills be hurled, let rocks be rent,
Let sun and moon grow dim.
When earth and hell their rage hath spent,
Thy soul shall dwell with him.

Let heav'n itself be in a blaze,
And time be past and gone.
Eternity shall hear our praise
Sound forth to God alone.

O make me Lord, through life and time,
And when I come to die,
Steadfast. Yea, let thy will be mine
On earth, and then on high.

For further reflection: Revelation 2:8–10

DAY OF REJOICING

Shout ye ransom'd, shout for joy,
For ye praise the Lord on high.
Praise his everlasting name,
For his saints his praise proclaim.

Tune your harps, make music rare,
Take your palms, your crowns now wear;
Sweep the strings, and let them raise
Everlasting hymns of praise.

Mount the chariot, ride along,
King eternal, hear the song.
Bow before him, bend the knee,
Christ o'ercame and set thee free.

Sweep the strings, again ye brides,
See the King of glory rides.
Heart and tongue, his name adore;
Praise and bless him evermore.

Crown the victor, crown the Lord,
Christ the everlasting word.
At his feet your trophies lay,
While ye live in endless day.

Jesus Conquer'r, to thy love
Every tongue in heaven shall move.
Angels, cherubim, and men,
Thy Love, shall all the host constrain.

FOR FURTHER REFLECTION: PSALM 24:9–10

PRAYER: KINDLE THIS HEART INTO A FLAME

Kindle this heart into a flame,
And make these eyes o'erflow.
Whisper but once thy sweetest name,
And then thy love bestow.

And when depress'd by direful grief,
Thy name my staff shall be.
It shall be all my help, and chief
My joy and liberty.

And then, when all this sorrow's past,
Still bear me in thine arms;
Where pleasures shall forever last,
Safely from all alarms.

O gracious Saviour, hear my prayer;
Help me while here I stay.
Give me on earth thy love to share,
And guide me in thy way.

And while I've breath still keep me near,
And teach me how to love
Aright that friend who paid so dear
To raise my soul above.

I know thy love for sinners Lord,
For thou dost love me so.
Then let me tell from thine own word
Thou lovest others too.

FOR FURTHER REFLECTION: 2 CORINTHIANS 1:3—5

CREATION

O Thou, who spoke and it was done,
At whose almighty word
Myriads of angels ever come
When thy great voice is heard,

Speak thou the word and let all see
Thy mighty pow'r to save;
Stretch forth thine hand that we may be
Snatch'd from th' Eternal grave.

Thou mighty Spirit, crush this will,
Conform it to thine own;
Make every step thy word fulfill;
The power is thine alone.

Come mighty Saviour, make us live
Above this dying rate;
Bid these cold spirits now to strive
Against this dying state.

Speed! Let the brightness of thy face
Illumine this cold breast;
Teach thou this heart to run the race
Until it finds its rest.

Then, might and honor, glory, pow'r,
We will ascribe to thee;
Thy praises shall through time endure
And through Eternity.

FOR FURTHER REFLECTION: 2 CORINTHIANS 4:3—6

OBEDIENCE

High as the highest angel stands,
There yet is mark'd on this seraphic being
Subjection to the Lord's commands
By all the starry host, his word obeying.

Obedience marks the greatest of them all;
And none throughout that brilliant throng,
Not one, attempts, though great or small,
To do the slightest thing that's wrong.

They all in strict obedience bow
At their Creator's nod;
In awful reverence lie low
And listen to his word.

Then with the light'ning's speed, they fly
To execute his word;
Perform the summons from on high,
His utmost word fulfill.

Then why should man of puny race
Be disobedient here,
And set themselves before his face
Refusing him to fear?

For by his breath, the summons came,
"Let man prepare to die."
Then mortals, come and fear his name,
For who can him defy?

FOR FURTHER REFLECTION: ISAIAH 6:1–3

18

HUMILITY

O Sovereign Giver, let us hear
Thee, speak in tones of love.
Come let us know that thou art near,
With blessing from above.

Make this proud heart before thee bow
And tremble at thy feet.
Lord lay me, and then keep me low;
'Tis for this state I'm meet.

This rebel heart will know no law
And all restraint defies.
Lord, send thy Spirit down to draw
My spirit to the skies.

Make me to feel I owe to thee
A debt I cannot pay.
Lead me in Jesus now to see
My sins are wash'd away.

Then make this treach'rous heart to feel
Humble, and low, and kind.
Apply the balm, and truly heal
What sin has left behind.

Wash me and make me white like snow,
Though crimson, white as wool.
And then the sinner, Lord, may know
Thee, as Bethesda's pool.

FOR FURTHER REFLECTION: JAMES 4:6–10

KING OF KINGS

O King of kings, thou dost bear rule
From sea to sea, from pole to pole.
Let thine own arm the victory get
Where'er the sun doth rise or set.

The hearts of kings are in thine hand
And all is thine in every land.
In every land, in every place,
Send down thy soul-subduing grace.

Make known thy word from sea to sea;
Let all the nations captives be;
Thine own almighty word proclaim,
Till earth shall echo Jesus' name.

Lord let the greatness of thy might
Be seen and heard both day and night.
Let every knee to thee be bow'd
And every heart by grace subdue'd.

Lord, let the whole creation ring
With praise to thee, the greatest King.
Let every nation own these words,
"Thou'rt King of kings, and Lord of lords."

Might, majesty belongs to thee;
All worlds perform thy great decree.
Praises beyond the earth's are thine,
From seraphs who in glory shine.

FOR FURTHER REFLECTION: PSALM 2:10–12

REJOICE IN TRIBULATION

Rejoice! Why art thou sad
And so cast down my soul?
Arise, lift up thy head,
For Jesus makes thee whole.

Why art thou so dismay'd?
Why sorrowing stand here?
All thy great debt is paid,
And Jesus calls thee near.

If thou art burden'd, come,
Taste of his gracious love;
See there thy future home,
The paradise above.

Come, cheer thy drooping heart;
Drink deeper of the well.
Jesus will bear his part;
To him thy troubles tell.

Come, lift thy voice and sing;
He set the captives free.
Thy sorrows to him bring,
And he will comfort thee.

His mighty voice shall sound;
The earth his voice shall hear.
Beneath or all around,
Nothing shall make thee fear.

FOR FURTHER REFLECTION: ISAIAH 61:1—2

21

ASHAMED FOR JESUS

Jesus, and shall it ever be
That I thy name shall scorn?
If there's a thought would trouble me,
'Tis this would make me mourn.

For I desire thy name to love,
Thy glory to adore.
O send thy Spirit from above,
And make me love thee more.

I'm oft in sorrow lest I stray
Away at last from thee.
Come, Jesus, to thy servant say,
"This thing shall never be."

For if thy love has once been giv'n,
Let it fore'er remain;
Let it secure my place in heav'n
Among thy glorious train.

Dear, constant, everlasting Friend,
Make this cold heart thine own.
O keep me to life's latest end,
And then, Lord, take me home.

Dear Jesus, let me grow in love,
And never let me fall.
And if I should begin to rove,
Dear Jesus, to me call.

FOR FURTHER REFLECTION: JOHN 10:27–30

43

GRACE

O Grace, I love this sound so dear
That all beside is dross.
Nothing removes my slavish fear
But Jesus and his cross.

Have I a thing that comes between
This precious grace and me?
Have I a sin I wish to screen?
Dear Savior, come and see.

And if thou findest aught not right,
Make it depart, I pray.
For Lord, I'm always in thy sight
And would not like to stray.

This grace is all my boast while here
And shall be always so.
This grace to thee has brought me near
And many others too.

Then Jesus, let thy grace supply
My every want in life.
Comfort and help me when I die
And part me from this strife.

And let me in thine arms be bourne
Away, where thou dost dwell,
Where mortals cease fore'er to mourn,
The song of heav'n to swell.

For further reflection: 1 John 1:6—9

SOVEREIGN LOVE

Thy love has kill'd this stony heart,
And made these eyes to weep.
To think that body bore the smart
That made the mighty deep.

O for such love, when thou could'st move
The empires with thy word.
But thou forborest thus, through love,
And did not use thy rod.

The whole creation at thy feet,
And yet, thou stoop'd and died.
The greatest love in thee did meet
When thou wast crucified.

O let this heart for such a gift
Be mov'd with holy fire.
O sacred Spirit, come and lift
This earthly heart up high'r.

And let the living strains begin
Higher than earth has heard.
Let me thy lasting praises ring
To Father, Spirit, Word.

These earthly words are far too weak
A love like thine to show.
Dear Saviour, though we cannot speak,
Let us its virtue know.

FOR FURTHER REFLECTION: ROMANS 5:6–8

PRAYER: LORD, LIFT THE CLOUD FROM OFF OUR SIGHT

Lord, lift the cloud from off our sight
That we may see thy face.
Let all the world behold thy might
And glorify thy grace.

For what is man if thou dost rise
To spread thy truth abroad?
Thou takest error from their eyes,
While they believe in God.

Then rise, O King of Grace, and spread
Thy truth throughout the world;
Unstop the ears and raise the dead;
Let error far be hurl'd.

Ride in thy chariot, through thy foes,
And bid the world revive.
Make men with mercy now to close,
And bid each dead one live.

Then all the world shall give thee praise;
Thy captives shall confess
Thy matchless pow'r, while they shall raise
Songs to thy righteousness.

And angels over men shall sing
And well behold with joy.
New themes throughout the heav'ns shall ring;
Seraphic tongues employ.

FOR FURTHER REFLECTION: REVELATION 7:9–11

ADORATION

In lofty strains, exalt your King;
In seraphic language, hail.
To him, the Lord, fresh honors bring;
Seraphs, angels, men prevail
To exalt this Lord of thine,
Who in glory is divine.

In holy raptures, let your soul
Raise his name above all else.
Make him of your thoughts the goal
And himself be all your wealth.
Let him be your heaven here;
His the only name that's dear.

In your song, let him be prais'd
And his glorious name be told.
Let highest strains on earth be rais'd,
And every mortal heart unfold
To receive our gracious God;
Dwell at last in his abode.

O, that some instructing Guide
To my joyful heart may come!
And bid me in his love confide,
Till I find myself at home.
There I'll never cease to love
God with all his saints above.

FOR FURTHER REFLECTION: PSALM 104:1—4

26

CHRIST THE ROCK (I)

Steadfast upon the Rock I stand,
Upheld by God's almighty hand.
In him I move, I live, or die,
In him I'll dwell beyond the sky.

Let worlds from nature's laws be cast,
In him I stand secure and fast.
Let heav'n and earth now pass away,
His hand shall guide to endless day.

When sun and moon their course have ran,
Or death arrives and I am gone,
Still I am safe, I know no fear.
His guardian hand shall then be near.

Shall judgment come with all its woe,
To stand before its bar, I go.
The judge, my friend, why need I quail,
When he has promis'd ne'er to fail?

O Solid Rock, thou can'st not move,
Thou can'st not take away thy love.
Fix'd and immoveable thou art,
Nor earth nor hell my soul can part.

Rock of my strength, my Jesus, God,
My soul is thine; I wait thy word.
Speak, and at once I'll gladly come;
Call me, I'll fly to thee, my home.

FOR FURTHER REFLECTION: 1 PETER 2:4–6

I Am the Way

There sounds a voice amid the crowd
Of mingled toil and strife.
"I am the Way" is heard aloud;
"In me there dwelleth life."

"Lost in this world, and prone to stray,
Hear ye the blessed news:
I am the Life, the Truth, the Way.
Come ye this portion choose."

Dark amid earth's entangled ways,
Without a ray of light;
Now let the dawn of brighter days
Begin to end thy night.

In nature's darkness, wrapt in gloom,
A light shines on the road.
It leads us to a glorious home,
To mercy, life, and God.

Lost amid traps and pitfalls deep,
The human race strays on.
In brazen chains of nature's sleep,
They pass the road along.

A light there is, they heed it not,
A path to endless bliss.
"I am the Way," they hear it. What!
They die refusing peace.

For further reflection: John 14:1–6

28

Prayer: Come, Sweetener of Our Earthly Cares

Come, Sweetener of our earthly cares,
And let us walk with thee.
Come, banish all our doubts and fears;
Make every sin to flee.

Thine do we wish to be, dear Lord;
But Satan with his snares
Is near when we attend thy word,
To sow his hurtful tares.

O, shut this heart against his wiles;
Make deaf these ears to him;
Make blind these eyes when Satan smiles;
Yea, shut me up from him.

For when alone with thee, my friend,
I long to hide awhile
From all that will thy grace offend
And all that may be vile.

Yet, still, the tempter will be there
To break my peace and joy.
Yea, night, and day, and everywhere,
He tries me to destroy.

O Lord, I wish to love thee more,
I hate his treach'rous arts,
And long to gain from thee the pow'r
To vanquish all his darts.

For further reflection: 1 Peter 5:8–9

WATCH

Watch! For the tempter plies his arts
And plans to make me fall.
His quiver, full of hellish darts,
He bears to wound my soul.

Watch! For the world and sin assail.
My soul stands shiv'ring here;
The strength I have begins to fail
And I am full of fear.

Watch! For the floods around me press
And troubles o'er me flow.
Help me whene'er I meet distress,
And make thy presence glow.

Watch! O my Friend, nor leave me now;
Be thou my help, my stay.
Before thy throne I humbly bow
And wish to love thy way.

Watch! And if aught but thy dear will
My soul inclines to do,
Make me to hear thy voice so still
And let me fear it too.

Watch! Through my life, and when I cease
This conflict to maintain,
Let my reward be endless peace
Alone through Jesus' name.

FOR FURTHER REFLECTION: EPHESIANS 5:8—14

HEAVENLY JOY

Hark! How in holy love
Men meet from every clime;
Enjoy the rest above
Beyond this scene of time.

There, joys eternal roll
Throughout the heav'nly plain;
From every heart and soul,
Their praises are the same.

No more in anger now,
They dwell in holy peace;
Before God's footstool bow,
Their love and joy increase.

Why should they here below
In anger speak a word,
And to each other show
Malice before unheard?

Why should the saints on earth,
Hastening to joys on high,
Be destitute of mirth,
While trav'ling to the sky?

Cease all your angry strife;
Of wars you have but one.
That lasts until your life
Shall end, and vic'try come.

FOR FURTHER REFLECTION: 1 CORINTHIANS 13:4—10

Holy Joy

In blissful mansions far away,
In holiness they rest.
Commenc'd that holy, happy day
Where mortals may be blest.

In yonder land of pure delight,
Without one dark'ning cloud,
They dwell in day, without a night,
To separate the crowd.

They join thy gracious name to praise
And spread thy wonders wide.
The glorious theme again they raise:
Jesus that lov'd and died.

With heav'nly songs, they sing thy name,
Thy deeds they still make known;
Throughout the heav'nly courts proclaim
The vic'tries of the Son.

Thus speed the hours of holy joy,
In praising Christ the Lord,
And in their gratitude employ
The sweetest heav'nly chord.

O, to be there to join their song!
I would this instant fly;
To see the glories of the throng
That dwells above the sky.

For further reflection: Revelation 21:22–27

BURDENED

Harden'd by sin, deprav'd with guilt,
Bound in chains of strongest brass;
Lord, thy precious blood was spilt
That my soul to heav'n might pass.

Though burden'd, yet thy soft'ning grace
Can make my burden soon to cease;
The darkest hour, thy lovely face
Makes my conscience feel at ease.

Fetter'd in chains of strongest sin,
Languishing in greatest pain,
Foes without, and foes within,
Jesus come, and come to reign.

Come quickly, Lord, and plead my cause,
Set thy love within my heart.
Teach me all thy holy laws,
Never let thy love depart.

Hold thou me high, this earth above,
Break the fetters, set me free.
Let me prove thy sovereign love,
Bid my heart rejoice in thee.

Belov'd by thee, I wait the prize,
Safely in thy blessed arms.
Raise me, Lord, above the skies
To behold thy lovely charms.

FOR FURTHER REFLECTION: PSALM 51:7—9

SABBATH (I)

Welcome sweet rest, which thy morning begins
To refresh me my journey to run;
That the snares and the dangerous path with its sins,
I may draw of his grace far to shun.

Bright morning, I hail; Sweet peace thou dost bring
To delight me, my course to pursue;
To the joys in reserve, where the ransom'd do sing,
Where my Lord's lovely face I shall view.

The region of bliss, that land ever bright,
Where the sunlight of God ever shines,
Where the joys, and the blessedness, and the delight
Of the glorified, ever confines.

This theme, my loftiest thought it requires;
To embrace it I cannot below.
'Tis too grand for this mind, and my highest desires
Ever fail its bright glories to show.

O my soul, 'tis for thee this reward,
'Tis the rest where the weary may stay.
Where amid gentle streams flowing out from our God,
We shall live through eternity's day.

Ah! Bright morn, thy sweet rest but reminds me
Of the rest that I soon shall enjoy,
Where, in peace passing thought, all the ransom'd I see
And join in their holy employ.

FOR FURTHER REFLECTION: HEBREWS 4:8–11

TEACH ME THY STATUTES
(PSALM 119)

Nine times oft repeated pray'r,
Lord, now the answer give.
Let all thy laws so wond'rous fair
In these our spirits live.

That statutes are our chief delight,
In all thy laws we find.
We get in each another sight
Of God the Father's mind.

To some thy laws may be a weight,
A burden hard to bear.
But not to us, who know our state,
They are as light as air.

Our Father, let us still repeat
This pray'r while we remain
On earth to learn thy path is sweet;
In heav'n to learn the same.

Where shall thy people find their joy
If not in thy dear will?
Then Saviour, let thy sweet employ
With joy our spirits fill.

We love thy peaceful paths on earth,
Which lead to joys above.
For all below is nothing worth
When plac'd beside thy love.

FOR FURTHER REFLECTION: PSALM 119:9–12

THOU SHALT NOT TAKE THE
NAME OF GOD IN VAIN

Thy name is far too sacred, Lord,
For mortals to profane;
A far too great and awful word
For men to use in vain.

Angels are awe'd when thou dost speak
And veil their faces too.
At mention of thy name, they seek
Thine utmost will to do.

And cherubim all bow to thee
And own thy gracious sway;
And none can in thy kingdom be
That dares to say the nay.

But harden'd man, thy word defies
And sets thy name at naught;
Against thy wise commandment flies
And turns thy will to sport.

The name at which the angels bow,
At which creation shakes,
Proud man disdains to hallow now;
Thy name in vain he takes.

But thou art fill'd with wond'rous love;
Thy sword thou wilt not draw,
But longs for him to rest above,
To learn to sin no more.

FOR FURTHER REFLECTION: EXODUS 20:2–7

JESUS' VOICE

Hark! These sounds strike some new chord.
In this heart, there seems to shine,
There spreads a thrilling of that word.
O Lord, hast thou just call'd me thine?

I mourn this faithless spirit,
Oft am vex'd for this my sin.
On thyself, my eyes Lord rivet;
O, this spirit Saviour win.

I feel my loss; this aching
Tells me thou hast gone from me,
And I feel an inward working,
A longing for thy face to see.

Jesus' voice has whisper'd peace;
Yes, his voice has quell'd my fear.
For all my doubts begin to cease
When Jesus' sovereign voice I hear.

Let thy brightest beams arise;
Sit where once there sat a cloud.
Come, Holy Spirit, from the skies,
Help me to sing thy praise aloud.

Come, thine hallow'd peace impart,
Cheer through every dreary day;
And with a cheerful loving heart
We will walk in wisdom's way.

FOR FURTHER REFLECTION: PHILIPPIANS 4:4–7

RECONCILIATION

Lord, let thy reconciling face
Shine forth to cheer each day.
Now let us all thy love embrace,
No longer to delay.

Let love constrain us in return
To take the offer'd hand,
Accept thy promises, and learn
To do thy blest command.

For since we left thy pleasant law,
We have no pleasure found.
The ways of sin have made us more
To hate its thorny ground.

We sought for rest, where there was none,
We sought for rest in woe.
Thy grace has led us to discern
Where peace and plenty flow.

And since we have engaged with thee,
And learn'd to do thy will,
Thou hast till now, and still will be
Our God, our souls to fill.

We now have peace, the world denied,
We find thy joys are great.
Pleasures flow down, a streaming tide
From heav'n's eternal gate.

FOR FURTHER REFLECTION: ROMANS 8:1–4

ASCEND

Mount! Leave this cumbrous clay;
Ascend beyond the sky,
Where reigns immortal day
And pleasures never die.

Then right beyond this state,
Where thou may'st draw thy breath,
There, thou thy Saviour's bidding wait
Without a fear of death.

Where no disturbing sound
Thy soul's delights to still;
In love forever bound
To do thy Maker's will.

Ah! Peaceful joyous land,
Thy pearly gates I see.
By faith I'm now among the band
In holy ecstasy.

O, to be there amid that host,
Safely among that throng,
Praising my great Redeemer most
With an immortal tongue.

Sick of the earth's best joys,
I pant to be with God,
To see my heav'nly choice,
And hear my blessed Lord.

FOR FURTHER REFLECTION: ISAIAH 66:22–23

ASK ME NOT TO STAY

Reason, why ask me here to stay?
Why urge thy pressing plea?
Let me now sing myself away
My blessed Lord to see.

Why make these anxious thoughts arise
Within this breast of mine,
And keep me down below the skies
In this low state to pine?

Friends, why desire me here to wait,
Immers'd in cares and woes?
Why keep me from yon happy state,
Amid a host of foes?

Cease all your pleading for me now,
Let me depart, I pray.
That I, at his blest feet, may bow
To spend that happy day.

After your plaintive cries for me,
Let this, your pray'r, ascend,
"Take him away to dwell with thee;
Lord, let his troubles end."

I know ye wish me here to dwell,
It cannot be for long.
Let me go now, that I may swell
That sacred heav'nly song.

FOR FURTHER REFLECTION: 2 TIMOTHY 4:6—8

PRAYER: JESUS, MY SOUL DESIRES TO SEE

Jesus, my soul desires to see
Thee as thou art in love.
For in this wretched state to be,
So far from thee above,
Is of all pains the worst to bear.
If in the furnace, thou wilt prove
Thy child, be thou then with me there;
Do not from me remove.

It matters not, if thou will stay
By me in all my trials here.
Let earth and hell their scepters sway,
I'll bear it all and feel no fear.
But if thou tak'st thyself away,
Sweet Jesus then I fall;
For nothing else can be my stay,
My Jesus, God, my all.

I long sought comfort in the world
And found that it was bare.
Until thy banner was unfurl'd,
My state was true despair.
But on thy loving breast I lean'd
And found true joy in thee.
Lord, from this world may I be wean'd
That I thy joy may see.

FOR FURTHER REFLECTION: ISAIAH 43:1—2

JUDGMENT (I)

In solemn state the Judge is seated;
Seraphs, angels, now rejoice,
For the Judge has call'd and greeted
All the people of his choice.

Angels bow, the ransom'd sing,
"Holy, holy, holy Lord,
Thou art worthy mighty King,
Victory to th' Eternal God.

Take immortal honors now.
Lo! Our crowns and palms we give.
Here before thee, now we bow,
And before thee, we will live.

Thou art worthy to be prais'd
Through that long mysterious time.
To thee all voices shall be rais'd;
Thou hast brought from every clime."

"Welcome to your lasting rest;
You have fought and conquer'd now.
Welcome to my loving breast,
As the ceaseless ages flow.

Angels, take the tares away,
Bind with everlasting chains
That throughout the endless day,
They may dwell in dying pains."

FOR FURTHER REFLECTION: REVELATION 20:11–15

ADDRESS TO THE WORLD

I am going, I am going, to be with the Lord,
For the pleasures to see that I read in his word,
With a host of bright seraphim leading the way,
Where the Lord of the heav'ns, his scepter doth sway.

I am going, I am going, forever to live,
Where the Lord has a glorious mansion to give
To them who are sav'd by the blood of the Lamb,
Who have trusted through life his victorious name.

I am going, I am going, where his glory doth shine,
Where forever and ever his love will be mine,
Where the saints rob'd in white forever say, "Lord,
Thou hast sav'd us from peril, and fire, and sword."

I am going, I am going, where God in his love
Reigns forever amid the bright host that's above,
Where in majesty awful, yet loving to me,
My Saviour's sweet face I forever shall see.

I am going, I am going, where some's gone before,
Who stand rob'd with their King, they unceasing adore,
Crying, "Thou, O dear Saviour, redeem'd us by blood
And made us all Kings and Priests to our God."

Let me go, Let me go, for I long to be there,
I pant for the love he has promis'd to share,
To see his sweet features, and lean on his breast,
To hear his sweet voice; Jesus, take me to rest.

FOR FURTHER REFLECTION: REVELATION 5:9B–10

Heaven Our Home (I)

While wandering in this world of woe,
What mis'ry we endure!
We look and fain would go
To heav'n's eternal shore.

When shall this world be done,
And all this trouble cease?
When shall we reach our home
And gain eternal peace?

Oft have we sought it but in vain;
We do not seek aright.
We have not trusted in his name,
Nor have we shown our light.

We look to all our friends
In all our troubles here,
But then we do not gain our ends;
It leaves us more to fear.

O lead us, Lord, to trust on thee;
Do thou our steps direct.
And in thy ways, lead us to see
That they are all correct.

O take us to our home
Where we shall see thy face.
Then we shall never, never roam
From thine all-powerful grace.

For further reflection: 2 Corinthians 4:16–18

Heaven Our Home (II)

Christian, look up! Thy portion is not here.
Thy home is yonder where there's peace,
Forever closed from fear.

Christian, why mourn? You're getting nearer home,
Where pleasures always near thee roam,
Where there can be no care.

Christian, rejoice! Thy mansion is prepar'd.
By all who love our Jesus,
This heav'nly home is shar'd.

Christian, why faint? Although the road is long,
'Twill end in triumphs and a song
That mortals never heard.

Christian, look up! Nor fear thy numerous foes.
The battle ends in victory
And terminates thy woes.

Christian, rejoice! The prize is all but won.
And trials, sorrows all but done,
And life is near its close.

Christian, hark! There's voices waiting there.
They wait but for a little while
Until the race is done.

Christian, behold! With outstretch'd arms they wait.
To welcome thee to rest,
They beckon thee to come.

For further reflection: Hebrews 12:22—24

PEACE

Thy sacred peace to us impart,
Give rest to every weary heart,
And make us feel thy tender care,
Still guide and keep us everywhere.

And if we stray away from thee,
Bring thou us back our sin to see;
Let true repentance then be giv'n,
And make us good and fit for heav'n.

We fall away from thee so deep;
We see our sin and scarcely weep;
We long to live thy precepts near,
And dwell in thee without a fear.

But in this world of sin we find
We fall so short, so far behind
What we would do; some wrong within
Rebels against to make us sin.

But while we sin, we grieve to do
Aught to offend a friend so true,
And pray for strength for future days
To keep us firm in wisdom's ways.

But all the power is thine, dear Lord,
To give us strength to do thy word;
'Tis thine to make us love thee more,
To make our hearts thy grace adore.

FOR FURTHER REFLECTION: ROMANS 7:18–25

SALVATION

Blow salvation through the earth;
Scatter peace, and joy, and mirth.
May the lands benighted long
Burst in loud triumphant song.

Making every heart to sing
Glorious praises to our King;
Sweep throughout this desert drear
Jesus' name, for all to hear.

And that they may to thee fly
Let thy love come from on high,
Making every heart to sing
Glorious praises to our King.

Speak, and make thy word to flow,
Conquer'ing sin and death below,
That the world in chains oppress'd
May obtain thy promis'd rest.

Making every heart to sing
Glorious praises to our King,
Then when earth and time decay,
Worlds like mortals pass away,

We may all be found in thee
Happy through eternity.
Then make every heart to sing
Glorious praises to their King.

FOR FURTHER REFLECTION: PSALM 67:1—4

My Way, My Truth, My Life

My gracious Saviour, thou art mine,
My way, my truth, my life.
Speak, Saviour, tell me I am thine,
And that shall end my strife.

Thy sacred name is all my boast
When doubts and fears assail,
And while I in that name can trust,
I shall with God prevail.

Fears I may have, but they shall flee.
Doubts may distress my soul,
But from them all I shall be free;
Thou, Lord, wilt them control.

O, that the world thy peace but knew
And saw thee once in love!
If they could once thy goodness view,
Their souls could ne'er remove.

Not for the world would we forego
The sweetness of thy grace;
Earth and its treasures, all we know
We'd leave to see thy face.

Treasures on earth, are nought but dross
When but compar'd with God;
Earth yields no comfort, all is loss
And can but pain afford.

FOR FURTHER REFLECTION: PSALM 73:25—26

WE GO ASTRAY

A rebel, far from thee I stray.
Without excuse I roam.
Nothing can now thy justice stay,
Or keep me from my doom.

I sin, yet know, t'will end in death,
And feel that death is nigh.
Before thee I will hold my breath,
Will but for mercy cry.

Where shall I go to seek for grace?
No helping hand I see.
A thick dark cloud obscures thy face,
And hides thy love from me.

But yet to Calvary I turn,
And there behold thy Son.
I see on him thine anger burn
For sins which I have done.

I hear him cry and yield his life,
"'Tis finish'd!" O, my Lord,
Has mercy conquer'd sin and strife?
Yes, Jesus, 'tis thy word.

I come, then, trusting in his blood,
I give my soul, my all.
I'll trust no other than my God;
Jesus, on thee I fall.

FOR FURTHER REFLECTION: HEBREWS 10:10–12

RELIGION

Thy ways are peace; thy paths are love,
Joy, pleasures, and delight;
A foretaste of the joys above,
The land with glories bright.

O Zion, still thy courts appear
To bear our souls away,
And when thy blest delights we hear,
We long to see thy day.

This earth sinks low when thee we view,
And all its joys decline;
And if thy glories we but knew,
Our thoughts would be sublime.

But while below, we cannot view
The beauties of the place,
Nor can we think what we shall be
When we shall see his face.

Nor eye hath seen, nor ear hath heard,
Nor hath it enter'd man,
To know the blessings thou hast stor'd
For those that love thy name.

But this we know, our mansions there;
Thy love awaits us all.
We'll gladly soar from earth and care,
When thou for us shalt call.

For further reflection: Hebrews 11:8–10

SACRAMENT (I)

Jesus, I come to take again
The emblems of thy death;
To think again of all thy pain
And of thy dying breath.

Torn by the cruel nails for me,
Can I forget thee now?
No, Saviour, that can never be;
I will before thee bow.

I'll wait in thine appointed way,
And see thee at thy board.
Come sit again, that I this day
May view my risen Lord.

O, while we taste thy precious blood
And feed upon thy love,
May we behold that precious flood
Our every sin remove.

Dear Saviour, come and break the bread,
Be present while we drink.
And while we see a Saviour dead,
Upon his death we think.

O Lamb of God, who died for us,
We celebrate the time,
When in thy death, there died the curse,
And made us to be thine.

For further reflection: Mark 14:22–25

REST

Rest! How sweet the sound to those,
Whose tot'ring, weary feet
Bespeak the pilgrim's early close
With life; to rest, how sweet.

To all on life's thorny road,
This sound their spirit cheers;
Whispers of peace, and great reward,
And end of all their tears.

Rest from the dark road below,
Where thorns lie thick and strong;
And from the turmoil here to go,
To join the heav'nly throng.

Beneath, the bright glorious skies,
Bound to this house of clay,
Waiting the summons for to rise,
And dwell in joyous day.

Yet, delights my soul can feel,
While thinking o'er my rest;
In yonder land there's balm to heal,
'Tis there I shall be blest.

Ah! Beyond this world I love,
Another brighter far;
A land of sweetest rest above,
Away from strife and war.

FOR FURTHER REFLECTION: ISAIAH 25:6—8

CHRIST THE ROCK (II)

My God, the rock on which I build,
My hiding place from every storm;
My every tempest here is still'd,
And all my trials here must calm.

On everlasting strength, I rest,
Serene while countless ills roll by;
In undisturb'd repose am blest,
While waves are rolling mountains high.

Surer than heav'n, this word must stand.
Beneath his eye the planets roll.
He speaks, and at his great command,
Nations or worlds must rise or fall.

But safe in him, I dwell in peace,
Encompass'd by almighty care.
Before his word my troubles cease,
And mountains are as light as air.

Solid, when worlds from space are torn,
And elements unus'd, decay,
When nations thrust from thee shall mourn,
And space and time shall pass away.

On thee I stand, my Rock, my God;
Secure I'll dwell before thy face.
Surer than heav'n, or earth, thy word
Shall stand when worlds shall have no trace.

FOR FURTHER REFLECTION: ISAIAH 55:10–11

THE WORLD'S EMPTINESS

In vain we search the world to find
Something to fill our souls.
This world has little that is kind;
It, like a desert, howls.

O Saviour, fill us with thy grace!
Let none be ours but thee.
Come Saviour, show us now thy face,
And then our wants shall flee.

This world is emptiness to those
Whose souls aspire above.
Its gold, and silver, is but dross
Beside thy precious love.

We need far more than all below
To satisfy our hearts.
We need thy love from heav'n to flow,
For that sweet peace imparts.

Earth and its riches we despise;
In thee our riches dwell.
Our waiting hearts desire to rise
Above, where all is well.

Depress'd and burden'd, here we stay
Till thou for us shalt call;
Till thou shalt bid us come away
To find thee all in all.

FOR FURTHER REFLECTION: ISAIAH 55:1–3

The Spring of Life

O God, the Spring of Life, to thee
I raise my earnest cry.
O, let my pray'r accepted be
With thee, beyond the sky!

I ask not life beyond my day,
'Tis not for wealth I crave,
'Tis this: that I may learn thy way,
That thou my soul would'st save.

Beyond what thou seest fit to give,
I do not ask for more.
But that in thee, I here may live
And learn to do thy laws.

This earth I would not wish to tread,
Immers'd in care and strife.
Yea Lord, I long to make my bed
In death, to gain thy life.

To be so far, and stay so long
Away from thee, my Lord,
I cannot; let me hear their song
And see their great reward.

Thou Spring of Love, I long to view
Thee, with thy ransom'd host;
The paradise thou'st bought anew,
For that which we had lost.

For further reflection: Proverbs 30:7—9

CHRIST OUR ALL

Our Father, Friend, Redeemer, God,
Our hope, our life, our joy,
Teach us thy way; thy blest reward
Shall give our tongues employ.

Shew us thyself, shew, dearest Lord,
The beauties of thy grace;
And let us in thy blessed word,
Behold thy shining face.

Reveal still more of all thy will,
The wonders of thy law,
And let us while with love we fill,
Behold thee and adore.

Awaken in this languid heart
A fire within to burn,
That may fresh energy impart,
Thy blessed truth to learn.

And while I read and learn of thee,
May sweetness fill my breast;
And while thy glorious truth I see,
May I upon it rest.

That, fill'd with knowledge, I may grow
In wisdom, love, and power,
And in my life thy love may show
Each day, yea, every hour.

FOR FURTHER REFLECTION: PSALM 119:17—19

HELP

Come! Enemies around me stand.
Plead thou the cause of those that fear thy name.
Uprise, thou Mighty One; thine host command,
From Zion, thy great deeds proclaim.

Foes press me sore; they plan my fall.
Awake, thou arm of strength! Scatter thy foes.
Hear thou when those that love thy mercy call.
Arise, their troubles now to close.

Come, for the danger threatens still,
And those that hate thy glorious name abound.
Earth, with her hatred, yet defies thy will.
Arise, her hatred to confound.

Prove to my faithless heart thy love;
Speak to my troubled spirit of thy peace
All that withholds my heart from thee remove,
And make these doubting thoughts to cease.

Lord, I am thine; then make me know
My sure foundation is thine holy word.
And to my spirit, still thy glories show
Such as poor mortals never heard.

Then, feeling all I have is thine
And thou art mine, while this short life endures,
Teach me thy love, O thou Power Divine;
'Tis but thy love, our soul assures.

FOR FURTHER REFLECTION: PSALM 22:22–24

YON BRIGHT WORLD

Yon bright world is beaming
With the fairest of delights.
Pleasures ever streaming,
My weary soul invites.

O, the blest reunion
Of God's ransom'd children there!
Ever blest communion,
These now have all to share.

Ah! Amid those beauties,
Never of the sight to tire.
Come, ye heav'nly duties;
Come crown, and golden lyre.

No night or shades to cloud,
The eternal year rolls on.
The ransom'd sound aloud
His praise in sweetest song.

Haste then glorious hour;
Speed on swiftest wings of love.
Give, O give me power
To swell their song above.

O, let me cease below;
Angels, let me soar away.
I'm waiting now to go
Upward to realms of day.

<small>For further reflection: Revelation 22:3b–5</small>

INGRATITUDE

O Lord, from whom all mercies come,
On whom we wait each day,
Alas, that we should ever roam
From love's own gentle sway.

From thy great store, our blessings flow;
Ungrateful can we be.
Make us, dear Lord, thy love to know,
Let that constrain to thee.

It grieves our hearts when we offend
Against thy holy law.
Our knees in deep contrition bend;
O, let it be no more!

Thy way make thou our chief delight,
Make us to love thy will.
And send thy comfort day and night
Our contrite souls to fill.

For from thine hand, we all receive
Health, peace, and holy joy.
Thy word alone, if we believe,
Will all our fears destroy.

Then may this happy state be ours
To feel that thou art near.
Our brightest days, or darkest hours,
Will bring us nought to fear.

FOR FURTHER REFLECTION: EPHESIANS 5:15–20

Come Ye Out from among Them

Quite separate, ye chosen of the Lord,
Ye stand amid a host of foes.
"Come from among them," is his word,
"In me ye find your sure repose."

No longer yours, but bought with Jesus' blood,
A price too great for man to pay.
Seeing your state, the Son of God
Came down and gave his life away.

Thy debt is paid, and all the price is giv'n,
To buy thee from a world of sin,
To bring thee at the last to heav'n,
And make thee reign in peace with him.

Ye stand distinct from all the world beside;
Ye are the purchase of his love.
He all your sins fore'er will hide,
And all your guilt fore'er remove.

Then if such heav'nly love be yours to know,
Live ye to higher joys than these.
And when the worldlings pleasures flow,
Touch ye them not, your Saviour please.

Earth cannot satisfy your high desires;
Heav'n can alone your spirit fill.
God all your effort here requires
To teach and live his holy will.

For further reflection: 2 Corinthians 6:14–16

Draw Us and We Will Run after Thee

Draw me, Jesus, from each sin;
Make me pure, my spirit win.
Make me now to love thy ways,
Serve thee all my earthly days.

Draw me, Jesus, make me mild,
Humble as a little child.
Never let me go from thee,
Till in heaven thy face I see.

Draw me, Jesus, from my care;
Make me trust thee everywhere,
Night and day to feel thy love,
Coming from thy throne above.

Draw me, Jesus, to thy side;
Let me in thy word confide,
Hand in hand with thee to go,
While I wander here below.

Draw me, Jesus, to the end;
In my trials be my friend.
Thou art ever mighty Lord,
Foes all flee before thy word.

Draw me, Jesus, to the sky;
Call me up to thee on high.
Leave me not so far to roam,
Far from thee, so far from home.

For further reflection: Hebrews 10:19–22

THY WILL BE DONE

Thy will be done on earth, my God,
By all the num'rous throng,
And every place where man hath trod,
Forsake each thing that's wrong.

And let thy kingdom come, O Lord,
Where'er thy mercies fall.
Let them attend thy sacred word
And on thy mercy call.

Say to each sinner, "Come to me,
Forsake your sins and live!"
Let all the world thy children be,
Thy spirit to them give.

Lead every lost one to thy throne,
The weary make thy care.
The sick, afflicted, bring thou home
Heav'n's best delights to share.

Come, Saviour, come, speak thou the word;
Our puny efforts fail.
Come, let thy sacred voice be heard,
Blow with salvation's gale.

Then shall thy will on earth be done,
Then shall thy glory flow.
Sinners from every land be won,
And heav'n with pleasures glow.

FOR FURTHER REFLECTION: EZEKIEL 37:11–14

HEAVEN (I)

Ah! Beauteous sight beyond this narrow sphere,
All toil and danger while I stay below.
There, parted from this world of fear,
Its cares, its troubles, never more to know.

Once safely pass'd beyond a world of sorrow,
In brightness far too great for mortal eyes,
Where dwells day, no thought of morrow,
Comes throughout, in yonder heavenly skies.

Cease, my heart, the land where thou shalt live is nigh;
A moment and thy waiting soul may speed.
A fear, a parting, then on high,
Earth pass'd, to brightest joys thy soul is led.

My soul, in all earthly cares, rest thou in him;
Lean on his arm in all thy troubles now.
Rejoice, while tribulations seem
To press thy spirit and to sink thee low.

Believe thou in him, who on earth's road once trod;
By earth forsaken, while all worlds were his.
The sun and moon well knew their God,
While man array'd themselves his enemies.

But lo! He rose, he lives, forever reigning.
Words send his angels, to our aid they fly.
We, when sun and moon are waning,
Shall reign immortal never more to die.

FOR FURTHER REFLECTION: HEBREWS 4:14—16

UNSEARCHABLE LOVE

Unfathomable depth, a mine yet unexplor'd,
Which knows no bottom, knows no bound;
Forth from its boundless tide is pour'd
A stream of love, with melting sounds.

Unbounded love, celestial spring of all my joys,
Of which I long to feel still more,
To wean me from these earthly toys,
The God of glory to adore.

I long to bathe still more in this blest sea,
And feel within, its sweet delights;
Always in its blest arms to be,
In brightest days, in darkest nights.

O, for to soar the height, to dive its deepest cave,
To stretch my wings across its span,
Immers'd within its boundless wave,
And all its sweet enchantments scan.

O, that the time were come, to bid me launch away;
In its embrace to close this scene,
In brilliant, life-inspiring day,
On Jesus' loving breast to lean.

Angel of mercy, cut the silvery cord
That keeps my spirit join'd to clay.
Angel of love, come, bring the word,
Say to my spirit, "Come away."

FOR FURTHER REFLECTION: PSALM 103:8—11

Sacrament (II)

A wretch, O Lord, to thee I come,
Unworthy of thy smile;
This desperate heart so prone to roam
And do each thing that's vile.

Come, Holy Spirit, cleanse away
The last remains of sin;
No more the prodigal to play,
But keep thy fold within.

O Lord, I come to thy rich feast,
To sit around thy board;
Of thy rich bounties for to taste
And view my risen Lord.

Thy blest repast thou dost provide
To cheer my weary soul,
That I may in thy love confide
And never more to fall.

Jesus, I take the emblems now
And think upon thy name.
In low humility, I bow
And clothe myself in shame.

I loathe the sins, by which I grieve,
My loving Lord and King.
O, make me always thee believe
And of thy glory sing.

For further reflection: 1 Corinthians 11:27–29

Nothing Shall Part Us

Should tribulations' fiercest rage
Against my soul be hurl'd,
My Father's honor will engage
To save me from a world.

Shall friends, acquaintance, me forsake
And pierce me to the heart;
Should enemies their counsel take
And thrust me with their dart,

I've more in thee than all my friends,
Thy love shall hold me true.
Enough in thee to make amends
And far eclipse them too.

My God, my Saviour, I am thine,
I give my heart to thee.
Thy Spirit tells me thou art mine
And nought shall vanquish me.

The storms are sent by thy command,
My trials come in love.
And strong amid them all I stand,
My strength is from above.

Why fear my soul to meet such cares
As God in wisdom sends?
In all thy troubles, conflicts, snares,
Almighty strength attends.

For further reflection: Romans 8:28–30

ABOVE THE WORLD

Smile on or frown,
It lasts but for a day.
And when that day is gone,
Both smiles and frowns decay.

Let hatred come,
This heart will not be sad.
It will but bring me home
To be for ever glad.

Light up the fires,
This soul can never burn.
'Twill kindle my desires
To see my Lord's return.

Let racks begin
Their cruel scourge again.
'Twill take me up from sin,
Where there can be no pain.

Let friends be few,
'Twill not my soul alarm.
God's strength is ever new
To keep from every harm.

Let death arrive,
He is to me a friend.
His stroke I shall survive
And then my troubles end.

FOR FURTHER REFLECTION: HABAKKUK 3:17–18

GO INTO ALL THE WORLD

Lord, to the world let me proclaim
The saving pow'r of Jesus' name,
That the whole world may loudly tell,
"Our Jesus hath done all things well."

He knows the world is sunk in sin
And knows that man can never win.
The prize he has for mortals earn'd
Until of Jesus they have learn'd.

O Lord, how long shall mortals stray,
Keep from thy loving arms away?
When shall the nations know thy law,
And learn of thee to sin no more?

O Father of our earthly bliss,
We will to all thy love confess.
Send us but aid to tell thy love,
To bring poor sinning souls above.

Speak to the tenderest thoughts of man
And show them thy salvation's plan.
Give them the pow'r to come to thee,
From sin, and death, and misery flee.

Bid them to thee, at last to rise,
Above these low, beclouded skies,
Where they may live without a pain,
Where mortals with their God may reign.

FOR FURTHER REFLECTION: 2 CORINTHIANS 5:18–21

68

FOUNTAIN FOR SIN

Fountain for sin, thine open side
For me from wrath fore'er to hide.
Glorious Redeemer, gracious Friend,
Hide me with thee until the end.

Guide me in peace, and make me pure,
Kept by thine hand, I dwell secure.
None may molest, no foe oppose,
If thou art near me, Sharon's rose.

None may accuse, my pardon sign'd,
Remains for me until the end.
Thou art my King, and none can dare
To take thy people from thy care.

Safely they dwell beneath thine eye,
Safely through life, and when they die,
Thou art their helper night and day,
And none can take their souls away.

Then our Redeemer still be near
To guard from hurt, to keep from fear,
To bid them from this earth to rise,
Triumphantly beyond the skies.

Call us then, Saviour, bid us come;
Call us away to be at home,
Where no disturbing thoughts assail,
At home with thee, within the veil.

FOR FURTHER REFLECTION: JOHN 3:14—17

Bethesda's Pool

C. H. Spurgeon, August 1862

The anxious crowd with longing eyes
The angels' first appearance wait.
He comes, but disappointment flies,
For all but one steps down too late.

But hope still lends her glim'ring light,
And nerves the sick ones still to try.
Beside Bethesda's pool at night,
The halt, the maim'd, and withr'd lie.

"Perchance though hitherto I fail,
This time the precious boon is mine;
That I with healthful voice may hail
And bless the institute divine."

'Twas thus that Israel's sick came down
And bath'd; mayhap, they might be cur'd.
The pool destroy'd, the angel flown,
In Christ our health is now restor'd.

And as Bethesda's pool, they saw
And step'd by faith beneath its flood;
Their sickness fled, whole as before,
So Jesus cleanses us by blood.

And though no pool, the Gentile race
Can fix their eyes on Calvary's mount,
And take the Saviour's offer'd grace:
Wash and be clean in this blest fount.

FOR FURTHER REFLECTION: JOHN 5:2–9

HE IS FAITHFUL

Thou Faithful One, whose promise stands,
Secure when storms and tempests rage,
E'en storms obey thy wise commands
And for our welfare must engage.

Amid a thousand ills, thy word
Makes straight a path thy love to show.
Amid earth's thunders may be heard
Thy gracious voice to us below.

Behind each cloud, thy face does shine
And well repays the passing tear.
For when we feel that we are thine,
It gives the death blow to our fear.

But how can I thus doubt again
Thy faithfulness, thy love, and grace,
If thou dost dwell in every pain,
Beside me, with thy gracious face?

Forgive, O Lord, this doubting heart,
And let me for the future see
How tender and how kind thou art
To all below, who trust in thee.

And if again this heart should faint,
Before the trials here I meet,
Hear, Lord, I pray thee my complaint,
And let thy love be calm and sweet.

FOR FURTHER REFLECTION: JAMES 1:12–15

WONDROUS LOVE

Amazing thought to fill the mind
And prove that God was wondrous kind:
He plan'd redemption by his Son
That sinners might by love be won.

And when the time was fully come,
Th' eternal Son with joy came down,
And with his life, the ransom paid
That men might sons of God be made.

Such wondrous love, surpassing thought!
Our God rebellious men has bought
And sav'd them for to sound his praise,
In sweeter notes than angels raise.

Such love, it melts these eyes to tears.
While viewing it I lose my fears,
And forc'd by silver cords to fall
I lose myself and find him all.

But what, for love so great, can I
Give him his laws to satisfy?
I give myself, 'tis all I have,
And trusting him, for mercy crave.

Still let me feel thy wondrous love,
And praise thee till I rest above.
On earth to thy great love I'll cling,
And when in heav'n, thy love I'll sing.

FOR FURTHER REFLECTION: JOHN 17:1–5

ANGELS REJOICE
OVER ONE SINNER

Hark! O my soul, some angel cries
As through the air with speed he flies,
With joyous news, "New gems are won
To sparkle in the Saviour's crown!"

The Spirit has, with touch divine,
Made some poor sinners to incline
To turn, to leave their galling chains,
Escape their doom and lose their pains.

Hear now in heav'n, with joy they sing,
Repeating triumphs of their King.
While every harp resounds aloud
That men to Jesus Christ have bow'd.

Awake, my heart, a victim torn
From paths of sin, and safely bourne
Within the fold, away from cares,
Beyond the tempter's traps and snares.

Vict'ry proclaim'd; love's gentle sway
Has torn from cruelty away
And plac'd beyond all fear, a gem
To glitter in Christ's diadem.

Speak, o ye kindred tongues above,
Echo the triumphs of his love,
From yon bright citadel to hear
How mortals fare, in yonder sphere.

FOR FURTHER REFLECTION: LUKE 15:1—7

I Count All Loss That I May Win Christ

I count all things but loss, for the grace of my Lord.
The richest of gold, I can find in his word;
A stream never ceasing, I have from the sea
Of the love of my Jesus that flows toward me.

All is loss that to gain the sweet joys of his grace,
And feel his love beam as it comes from his face,
And know, as I hear and approach to his love,
How intense are the joys he has bought me above.

On this earth, there is nought that can offer supplies
To meet with my wants, or to gladden mine eyes.
All dross, all is vanity, nothing while here;
In striving to grasp them, they all disappear.

But in Jesus, I find all is real and bright;
A star to illumine my long weary night,
A voice that in danger makes foes flee away,
And from gloom in an instant turns night into day.

A strong shield, and a buckler, a captain whose arm
Is made bare for defense, to keep from alarm.
A friend who can see all my foes drawing nigh
And whose word in an instant can make them to fly.

All things else sink below this great friend in my view.
He cannot for worlds prove a moment untrue.
All things that in time or eternity are,
O no, nothing can I with my Jesus compare.

For further reflection: Philippians 3:7—9

To Die Is Gain

For me to die is gain,
To be by Jesus' side,
To know no sorrow, feel no pain,
In Jesus' love to hide.

Always before his face,
And hear the host proclaim
The sweetness of his saving grace,
The glories of his name.

O, to be at his feet,
Learning still more of him;
To see the num'rous armies meet,
And bow before their King.

Could I this moment view
In robes of light divine;
Could I but pierce the curtain through,
And see how mortals shine.

This spirit could not stay
Away from such fair scenes;
I'd cast this earth and all away
To be where Jesus reigns.

O, sweetest hour of time
That brings me to the gate
Of death, and bids me enter in
To everlasting state.

For further reflection: Philippians 1:21–26

O Lord, How Long?

O Lord, how long? The many ills
That vex our souls, rise swelling like the sea.
Thy word our anxious spirit fills,
And bids us dying look to thee.

O Lord, how long? Storms rage around
And darkness gathers o'er the path we tread.
Alone amid the desert, found
Helpless, our hearts the dangers dread.

O Lord, how long? Thy face is hid;
The light is out that once we used to view;
Thy spirit gone that ever bid
Us trust thee, and adore thee too.

O Lord, how long? Thy smile withdrawn
That lit the path when darkness seem'd to reign,
And bid our hearts no longer mourn,
Our loss shall be eternal gain.

O Lord, how long? Till death's cold hand
Come with thy word to bid us soar away,
To see thy face where angels stand
And worship thee in endless day.

O Lord, how long? Till glory shine,
And heav'n reveal'd, bids us to join the song;
When thou shalt call us ever thine,
And we shall say no more, how long?

For further reflection: Psalm 13:1–3

PRAYER: O LOVE, ON WHICH MY HOPES I REST

O Love, on which my hopes I rest,
And trust thee with my soul,
Whose tender heart, whose loving breast,
Will never let me fall.

While here, and when I pass from time,
Thou art my friend, my guide;
In dangers, sorrows, thou art mine,
Keep very near my side.

When in the world I meet distress,
And foes my progress stay,
Thy voice makes all my troubles less
And leads my foes away.

And where but to thee can I come?
Thou hast the words of life.
A word from thee shall soothe and calm
And soften every strife.

Ah! Lord, thy name bestows on me
A peace and joy so deep.
So great a love I find in thee,
In gratitude I weep.

For this rich love no mortal tongue
Can speak with equal praise.
Above, we'll try to join the song
That ransom'd spirits raise.

FOR FURTHER REFLECTION: PSALM 130:5–7

PRAYER: ARISE, AND LET FRESH SIGHTS OF THEE

Arise, and let fresh sights of thee
Our thrilling souls revive;
And give us thy bright face to see,
And for thy likeness strive.

O Lord, without thy light, we die;
Without thy heav'nly face,
We sink beneath a frowning sky
And die for lack of grace.

But shall thy promise fail us now
When we so long have found
Thy word secure? Wilt thou allow
Our pray'rs to be but sound?

No, this can never be thy will;
Nor shall it e'er be heard
Thy promise thou wilt not fulfill
Or fail of thine own word.

Earth and its scenes may pass away,
And heav'n be pass'd from view,
Still thine own word shall hold the sway
And prove that thou art true.

Then, if thou art in strength the same
As tender in thy love,
Teach us to trust thy holy name
And wait thee from above.

FOR FURTHER REFLECTION: HEBREWS 6:17–19A

Prayer: O Lord, Let All the Nations Say

O Lord, let all the nations say
That thou art God supreme.
Let holiness protect their way
That own thee for their King.

For thou dost give them all their food,
Supply'st their every need.
They have from thee their every good;
The heathens thou dost feed.

Then why should they not own thy name
And give the praise that's due?
For by thy word the nations came,
And all their mercies too.

O, let them all confess thy love!
Give grace to make them feel.
Shower down thy blessings from above,
And teach the world thy will.

That they with us may gain thy rest
That thou so free hast given,
That they, by thee, may all be blest
At last, with thee in heaven.

Great God, let chains forever cease,
Let unity prevail,
That holiness and joy and peace
May make them cease to wail.

For further reflection: Acts 17:24—27

REJOICE

Christian, rejoice to sing
The praises of your God!
Let all your voices ring
The triumphs of his word!

My soul desires to love,
And see that lovely form
That waits my soul above,
My troubled heart to calm.

In high and glorious light,
With God fore'er to dwell,
In Jesus' blessed sight,
Their numbers for to swell.

Without a cloud between,
His face fore'er to view,
Amid yon happy scene,
With pleasures ever new.

In likeness we shall grow,
Never to fall again,
In adoration bow
To Jesus, who was slain.

My God, let me be found
Ready to enter in,
When trumpets' lovely sound
Shall call me up from sin.

For further reflection: 1 John 3:1–3

HEAVENLY JOYS

The strains I hear, but they are higher,
Far exceeding all my thoughts.
To that land I must aspire,
Tread at last those heavenly courts.

The joys of earth I feel are worthless,
Not to be compar'd with heav'n.
None approaches real greatness,
But the joys that God has giv'n.

I know the earth is full of treasure,
But in grasping them they flee.
Cares and tumults without measure
Is the portion giv'n to me.

But the thoughts of better things
Cheers my soul through every ill,
And the voice from heav'n brings
Sweetest joys my soul to fill.

In every joy on earth, there's pain;
In every pleasure, there's a thorn.
For all the treasures here are vain,
A moment's joy, a day to mourn.

But in that region, pleasures flow
That may fill th' mortal breast.
Higher joys our souls shall know
In that sweet and peaceful rest.

FOR FURTHER REFLECTION: ROMANS 8:18–23

GRACE GAVE ME TO GOD

With sighs and tears, this vale I've trod,
But grace has giv'n my soul to God,
And he has taught me who to fear
And made me trust a Saviour dear.

My brightest hopes are far away,
My choicest treasures ne'er decay,
In scenes so grand surpassing thought,
Where sweetest music may be caught.

Though in this vale we've little joy,
We pass from earth to sweet employ.
Nor tired amid yon heav'nly throng,
We'll join the never-ending song.

Earth has its pleasures, which are few;
Heav'n has its treasure ever new.
And though on earth we may have tears,
We leave at death the source of fears.

Earth has its love, though faint it be,
T'will be eclipsed when him I see.
When on his love-encircled throne,
I shall know full, as I am known.

Why am I kept in this low state,
So long from thee on earth to wait?
Hasten the time, my Jesus Lord,
Hasten to bid me rise, my God.

FOR FURTHER REFLECTION: MATTHEW 6:19–21

Behold, I Am with You Always

O Lord, the word we have proclaim'd
Is thine. Then make it grow
To make thy goodness to be fam'd.
Let thy salvation flow.

Let all the seed spring forth and bud;
Let none be sown in vain.
Make every seed produce some good,
And thou shalt glory gain.

For our best effort is to plant
The seed that it may spring,
That it may grow, dear Jesus grant,
And it shall glory bring.

The word is thine, the pow'r is thine
To sow and make it live.
In every heart, send grace divine,
And they their hearts shall give.

In heav'n we shall behold the sheaves,
Which thou hast gather'd in.
Behold the many olive leaves,
Which thou hast pluck'd from sin.

But gracious Father, let us see,
Thy word is growing now.
Receive, O Lord, this humble plea,
Come, let salvation show.

For further reflection: Matthew 28:18–20

Our Shepherd

On a hill, a shepherd sat watching his flock,
To keep them from danger and harm.
And reining them into the fold with his crook,
He guards them from every alarm.

At shades of the evening, he gather'd them in
And thus kept them from fear and assault.
In his arms, he would bear all the weak and the thin,
The sick with the maim'd and the halt.

His care was to keep every danger away,
To keep them in paths that were right.
And to keep all the lambs that were likely to stray,
His care reach'd from morning till night.

And thus, does the Shepherd of Israel's sheep
Defend them from harm and distress.
In safety he has and always will keep
The sheep who his care will confess.

He keeps them amid all the storms of this world,
And can never allow them to fall.
His foes from his face will forever be hurl'd,
While his sheep to his arms he will call.

Against them not one in the world shall prevail,
Nor molest through that long happy time.
In safety they all with the Shepherd shall dwell,
When his sheep come from every clime.

For further reflection: John 10:11–15

The Greatness of God's Love

O Lord, thy love is past our pow'r;
To know it full we never can;
To know its height, and depth, and breadth,
It is not given to mortal man.

Let it suffice, thou lovest us,
And thy great love can never change.
Lord 'tis enough that we are thine,
And nothing can thy love infringe.

Let my whole life be spent for thee;
Let not another claim my love.
And let the world take knowledge that
My life is hid with Christ above.

Our days, our hopes, thou know'st them all;
First and the last, thou art to us.
Thou hast remov'd all sin and fear,
And brought us on thy name to trust.

Then let me to the end endure
That I may soon be found at home.
Let every trial make me say,
"Thy will on earth with me be done."

I long to feel thee ever nigh
And know thy love, and see thy face.
In yonder sphere of love and peace,
To know my Saviour and his grace.

For further reflection: Ephesians 3:16—19

FEARFUL OF SINNING

Why, my soul affrighted, dost thou shrink away?
What whisper's that which made thee start?
And why look'st thou in such dismay?
And what is this that pains thy heart?

Hast thou then learn'd to hate this cursed thing,
To tremble at the look of every sin?
And dost thou long the sinner for to bring
The courts of peace and holiness within?

And does the least approach of sin alarm
Thy tender conscience, and thy soul offend?
And seest thou the greatness of the harm
They do, who all their lives in sin do spend?

And has the brightness of th' Eternal Sun
Shone on thy long-benighted soul at last?
And the new race, hast thou commenc'd to run?
Are all things new, old things forever past?

Then art thou blest, for everything thou hast,
Riches and pow'r, honor, might and love.
Thy sins in deepest seas forever cast
Henceforth remains for thee the joys above.

Eternity shall roll, and time be dead,
And all things past that thou beholdest now.
But thou shalt wear upon thy head
A crown, shall deck thy ransom'd brow.

FOR FURTHER REFLECTION: PHILIPPIANS 2:12—13

INASMUCH AS YE DID NOT DO IT UNTO THESE MY BRETHREN

When hungry, cold, forlorn I stray'd,
Was buffeted and scorn'd.
By every one was mock'd, betray'd,
No heart with pity warm'd.

Thirsty and tired I wander'd wide,
Deserted, shun'd, oppress'd
With none to stay my sorrows tide,
Or help me when distress'd.

But now you sue for mercy's hand
To be outstretch'd to you.
The wicked out of every land
Wish to escape their due.

"O Lord, we never saw thee thus
And never clos'd our door
Against thy mar'd, but glorious face,
When thou wast very poor."

"Yes! Inasmuch as thou didst do
These things to all my sheep,
Accept the portion due to you
Eternally to weep.

With racks, and fires, and hatred strong,
Your cruel vengeance spread.
But now, I visit all their wrong
Tenfold upon your head."

FOR FURTHER REFLECTION: MATTHEW 25:41—46

CHILDISH CONFIDENCE

Childhood, sweet innocence, claiming our love,
Entwining thine heart round our own.
Thou art surely a gift from our Father above,
From the Father of Spirits a boon.

O, that thy childlike behaviour was mine,
That in innocence I might be here.
From every sin my heart to refine
And make my profession sincere.

I leave this low state too often I know;
This proud heart desires to soar.
Not content with my lot, alas, I do show
I love this poor world all the more.

O, that I could dwell in humility now,
A child thy dear will to obey;
That before thy command I always could bow
And be led by thine hand all the day.

Then take from this heart every thing that is wrong,
And make me a child in thy ways.
'Tis to gain this low state that my spirit does long,
And then thy dear name I will praise.

For I long to be led by thine hand, and be kept
From the slippery paths of this road.
Until I, in thee, shall at last having slept
And passed from the earth to my God.

FOR FURTHER REFLECTION: MARK 10:13—16

Thou Knowest Us Altogether

In every scene of deep distress
Through which the Christian goes,
This comfort makes his sorrows less:
The Lord our trouble knows.

'Tis he that form'd, and brought us here
And still sustains us now;
'Tis he who planted first his fear
And made his love to flow.

And he our every step attends
And guards them while they rove.
'Tis he the broken heart that mends
And heals their wounds with love.

And if in sin their feet does slip,
His pitying heart pleads thus,
"O Lord forgive these straying sheep
Until they dwell with us.

Look not on them but thy Son;
They're mine, thou gav'st them me."
O Jesus, let thy mercy come;
O plead awhile for me.

Guide me until I gain the height
Where I may see thy face.
Keep me until I get a sight
Of the rewards of grace.

For further reflection: John 17:6–10

Metropolitan Tabernacle Dedicated

O Lord, another house is rear'd
Where thou delight'st to dwell.
Let thy dear name be here revered;
Here, let thy praises swell.

In adoration, Lord, we bow
For what thine arm has wrought.
Thy strength here to thy people show,
Nor let us know a drought.

Let plenteous showers of grace divine
Forever here descend;
May in this house thy glory shine,
And every one attend.

Whene'er thy servant speaks thy word,
Let every heart be lent.
Whene'er thy word resounds, dear Lord,
Let sinful hearts repent.

Here, let thy thirsting people live
Alone beneath thy care.
Let saint and sinner here believe,
And every blessing share.

This house is thine; 'tis raised for thee
And dedicated to thy praise.
Let holiness its portals be,
And in this house bestow thy grace.

For further reflection: Ephesians 2:19–22

Before the Mountains Were Brought Forth, Even Then Thou Art God

Before the dark terrestrial ball
Away in ether flew;
Before it heard its Maker's call,
Or his great voice it knew;

Or when in proud delight there dash'd
The various orbs unseen,
In careless majesty they crash'd
Against each other then;

Or long ere any orb was form'd,
When darkness held the sway;
When neither one nor other roam'd
Throughout the dismal day,

Even then in solemn state, there dwelt
In some far point in space,
Th'eternal God throughout was felt
And own'd in every place.

For but a word resounds abroad,
The elements appear
Before the majesty of God
His summons for to hear.

Words made the worlds, they built the sky;
He spoke 'twas done they firmly stood.
He look'd below and look'd on high
And said the whole was very good.

For further reflection: Genesis 1:14—18

Dying Saviour

Oh, thou lovely dying Saviour,
On the cross I view thee now.
O, let my sincere endeavour
Be to crown that glorious brow.

Not with thorns, my lovely Jesus,
Nor derision would I place
On that brow that bow'd to save us,
On thy mar'd but lovely face.

Not with mockings would I hail thee,
Nor with taunting words I'd pain,
But with heart devout, sincerely
Reverence thy holy name.

Make me here to stay in love,
Adoration, wonder, praise.
Let thine words be heard above
As this sacred hymn I raise.

Jesus, thou hast paid my debt;
Let this heart remember thee.
On the cross, with bloody sweat,
Thou didst pay the price for me.

And am I thine, this heart thine own,
Purchas'd by thy precious blood.
'Twas this black heart that made thee groan;
Thou shalt have it, Jesus, God.

FOR FURTHER REFLECTION: MATTHEW 27:27–31

He Sees Everything

There's not a sparrow down can fall,
But by his eye, 'tis seen;
And not a creature to him call
But he knows what they mean.

The lion and the tiny ant,
They all receive from him;
The stoutest oak, the smallest plant,
Depends upon its King.

The word that bid the light exist
And made the stars above,
The same by whom all things consist,
By him all creatures move.

In old eternity he dwelt
And treasured up his wind;
And he who makes the mountains melt,
The sea with bands confin'd.

There's not the smallest atom here
But by his word 'twas form'd.
He speaks, the billows quake with fear,
The raging sea is calm'd.

He made them all to wander here,
But for a time to stay.
But man, he made that he might fear
His greatness day by day.

For further reflection: Job 38:4—7

EMPTINESS

Again we come, our oil is out;
Our empty souls we bring.
Lord, sweep away all fear and doubt
And own a worthless thing.

We leave the world to come and taste
Of all thy blessings, Lord.
And what we hear, lets hold it fast,
And treasure up thy word.

In all thy courts, thou tak'st delight
And mak'st thy love appear.
We come to gain another sight;
Lord, let that sight be here.

Fresh oil into our vessels pour
And make our lamps to burn.
And let thine heav'nly graces show'r
Wherever we may turn.

O Lord, thou knowest our constant need
Of grace to help us on,
And grant that we may always feed
Upon the Holy One.

We faint, we droop; without thine aid
Our light is dying fast.
O come, thou Sacred Spirit, speed,
And make our light to last.

FOR FURTHER REFLECTION: 2 CORINTHIANS 1:8–10

HE IS OUR HELPER

In every stage of life, we feel
His shadow o'er us cast,
And faith assures he cannot fail
To own us at the last.

Why sinks this heart when things look dark?
'Tis then he's near us most.
The lightning's flash, the Spirit's spark
Shall terrify a host.

Chariots about his people move;
In strength divine they're clad.
Open these eyes to see thy love,
And make these spirits glad.

Why should the heirs of heav'n wear frowns?
'Tis not for them to cry.
"Rejoice, my people, there are crowns
For you to wear on high.

These enemies of thine shall know
That I will vengeance take;
And let eternal anguish flow
On them for your sake.

For you have known my holy name
And kept my statutes too;
And trembled lest you should profane
The laws I gave to you."

FOR FURTHER REFLECTION: PSALM 42:9–11

REFLECTION

Another week has borne our sins
Up to the Father's throne.
O, that the Lord these hearts would cleanse
And bid us cease to mourn!

Our sinful souls are very weak
Temptation to withstand;
Grant us thy pow'rful aid to seek,
And give a helping hand.

We know full well the tempter's wiles;
The stratagems he tries.
With frowns and hatred or with smiles,
His wicked arts he plies.

And only in thine armour clad,
We're proof against his dart.
In every path his snare is laid
For this too willing heart.

But clad in such a coat of mail,
We need not fear his rage.
Whene'er the tempter doth assail,
Thy strength we may engage.

O gracious God, make bare thine arm
To help thy people now.
Scatter all fear and all alarm
That we thy strength may know.

FOR FURTHER REFLECTION: EPHESIANS 6:10—12

Reasoning with
the Sinner

Come, sinner; let's reason your case to the end.
Let's endeavour to show you your state,
Before all the time you are given, you spend,
And before you can call it too late.

You have sinned and the end of that sin will be death,
And how soon you may die you can't tell.
And if but the Lord should desire your breath,
You will sink at once straight into hell.

You have had all your mercies at present on trust,
And for none of them all have you paid.
If you die as you are, from God you'd be thrust,
And the debt on your soul will be laid.

Mercy's offer'd and if you but take it today,
Your soul will forever be lov'd,
Your conscience be clear, your sins wash'd away,
And the stains of your guilt be remov'd.

The message is simply, "Believe on the Lord,
Salvation is for you procur'd."
Believe then on Jesus, and trust in his word,
And then your salvation's secur'd.

And angels with joy shall bear the good news
Of a sinner returning to God,
Of one who will now no longer refuse
To tread in the heavenly road.

For further reflection: Isaiah 1:18–20

THEY THAT RUN IN
A RACE, RUN ALL

The race is mark'd, and all may run,
All may engage who will.
Some have at once this race begun,
While some are standing still.

But why do they not get the prize,
'Tis offer'd to them all?
'Tis shown before their open eyes
While they refuse the call.

Some in every age have gain'd
The prize, have bourne [*sic*] away
The race through life; they have maintain'd
And won the well-fought day.

But some would never strive nor try
To enter in the race,
And would not at God's altar cry
To him for running grace.

And yet, they all expect the crown;
Their expectations vain.
Instead of striving, they sit down
And would not it obtain.

They will not come and serve me here,
But yet they ask reward.
They ask for heav'n, without a tear,
A heaven without a God.

FOR FURTHER REFLECTION: 1 CORINTHIANS 9:24–27

Conqueror

Come, thou mighty conqueror,
Come thyself to slay thy foes.
To the world their state discover,
While thy mercy's river flows.

Point them to thine open side,
Jesus' love and righteousness.
Shew them each the crimson tide;
Each rebellious sinner bless.

Make them to succumb to thee;
Make them all to see their wrong.
Lead them all the blood to see;
Gather all the guilty throng.

Here are eyes, but blind they are;
Here are ears, but deaf they seem.
Wake them ere they go too far;
Wake them up from nature's dream.

Rouse them let them see their state;
Let them flee while there is time.
Shew them what will be their state,
If thy mercy they decline.

To each wand'ring one return;
Make them to thy bosom fly,
Lest they should but live to burn,
Where the worm can never die.

FOR FURTHER REFLECTION: EPHESIANS 2:4—9

MIGHT

Not may, nor can, but shall and will.
The Lord delights to use,
Not giants does his word fulfill,
Nor mighty men he'll choose,

But feeble instruments he takes
To strike his mighty blows.
The greatest foe a friend he makes;
By love he overthrows.

A city at his voice shall fall;
A host to him shall yield.
Not arms, nor thunderings, nor hail,
His word shall clear the field.

And in his grace he but demand,
His foes at once they quail,
And hard rebellious heathen's lands
Upon his name shall call.

He speaks and all his foes dismay'd,
Trembling to him, they cry,
"Oh, Jesus, all our sins here laid."
In love, their tears they dry.

Once rebels, but thy pow'rful hand
Subdued and made them thine,
And brought them out of every land
In thine own crown to shine.

FOR FURTHER REFLECTION: 1 CORINTHIANS 1:26–29

LOVEST THOU ME?

Do I love my Saviour much?
'Tis much I ought to love.
He bought me, an unworthy wretch,
A place with him above.

I love him, but not half so well
As his first love deserves.
Dear Saviour, I with sorrow tell
I make such great reserves.

But Lord, forgive, and make me bold
To own thy glorious name.
No more, O Lord, let me grow cold
Or have the slightest shame.

For thou hast done such thing for me,
Hast liv'd, and bled, and died.
E'en now thy mercies, Lord, I see,
And yet not satisfied.

O Lord, this heart will never love
Until thou it subdue;
Until thou every sin remove
And mold it e'er anew.

And make it like thyself once more,
Thine own commands to do.
And then I will thy name adore
And love thy statutes too.

FOR FURTHER REFLECTION: JOHN 21:17—19

Missing God's Presence

Where is the smile I oft have felt?
Where fled that lovely beam,
To tears which made this heart to welt?
Come back, thou lovely gem.

Still make this heart to be thy place,
Where thou delight'st to dwell.
My every doubt and fear to chase,
And every cloud dispel.

Let no disturbing cares assail
This breast, but let me know
Thy brightness, dear Immanuel.
Thy love and glory show.

Let no unfeeling thoughts of thee
E'er harbour in this heart.
And always when thy face I see
Thy likeness, Lord, impart.

And let thy cheerful spirit stay
And hover round my face.
In all thy providence portray
Thy likeness and thy grace.

That I each day may do thy will
And lean upon thy breast.
Thine utmost law, I may fulfill
And in obedience rest.

For further reflection: Psalm 51:10–12

THOU ART THE
KING OF GLORY

O King of glory, take thy place
In this deceitful breast.
Come, King eternal, plant thy grace,
And let that give me rest.

Why wilt thou let a rival reign
Or sit upon thy throne?
Why let a traitor honor claim?
Come reign thou here alone.

This heart was not for Satan made;
'Tis thine, Creator, thine.
Speak thou the word, and when he's fled,
There let thine image shine.

This throne is sacred to thy name;
Who should usurp its seat?
Let all who to this seat lay claim
With thy displeasure meet.

Then take thy place in this thine heart,
And sway thy sceptre there.
And let thy reigning grace impart
The knowledge of thy care.

That neither life nor death may tear,
Nor anything begin
To separate me from the care
Of him that dwells within.

FOR FURTHER REFLECTION: DEUTERONOMY 6:4—9

THOU ART OUR STRENGTH

Strong Arm, outstretch; the victory take.
Who can before thee stand?
From every place new captives make
By thine almighty hand.

Defeat the treach'rous, artful foe;
Enlighten every mind.
Let heav'n and earth forever know
The pow'r is thine to bind.

But loose the fetters, break the cords,
Set every mortal free;
That all the world may of thy word
Learn true humility.

Make seraphs, angels, men to sing
Deserved honors now.
Let cherubim proclaim the King,
While men and angels bow.

'Tis thine, Creation's at thy feet,
Ready at thy command.
The universe in thee does meet,
Much more this smaller land.

Then speak, command thy grace to flow.
And clear the world of sin
That every nation now may know
Thy pow'r, to bring them in.

FOR FURTHER REFLECTION: ISAIAH 49:5—6

The Firmament Sheweth His Handywork

The wondrous orbs declare thy fame;
Thy doings they make known.
E'en the dumb planets praise thy name,
And thy control they own.

The sun, and moon, and stars repeat
The greatness of thy pow'r.
And all creation, now complete,
Thy wondrous name adore.

Where through the vast extent of space
Is there an orb that stands?
And negligent to run its race
Resists thy great commands?

Let thousand worlds before thee roll
In majesty sublime.
Ten thousand more, if thou dost call,
Will in a moment shine.

Through space there none betrays a breath
Against the name of "Yah."
And why should man so close to death
Thine awful greatness dare?

Where is the help for sinful man
Except it be in thee?
And who is there on earth who can
Resist thy firm decree?

For further reflection: Psalm 19:1—4a

Hear Infants' Praise

Bend down thine ear; catch this faint praise
That infant voices give.
Hear, Lord, the prayer they try to raise
And bid each infant live.

They try from their poor lips to send
Thy goodness very high.
Then to the young, thy love commend;
Give blessings from on high.

Make every little heart to know
Thou lovest every one.
Now to them all salvation show,
And bid them all to come.

In days gone by, thou didst desire
Them to be brought to thee.
Come, Holy Love Inspiring Fire,
And teach sincerity.

That they may all thy blessing feel
And thy salvation know;
Permit, dear Lord, this last appeal:
Save them from endless woe.

Young in the paths of sin, they stray;
O, let them fear thy law,
And after time, in endless day,
Thy wondrous grace adore.

For further reflection: Matthew 19:13–15

Come unto Me

"Come, ye sin sick souls; receive
The message of your God."
O Lord I hear, I would believe,
I would obey thy word.

But this foul soul of mine is lost.
If thou wilt let it be,
Amid the tempests to be toss'd,
It will not come to thee.

O Lord my weakness I have prov'd,
I faint, I sink, I die.
Lord let my sin be all remov'd;
This is my only cry.

My heart's distress'd about my lot
In thy great joys above.
Lord, let my sins fore'er be blot
Out by thy sovereign love.

This, this poor shiv'ring heart may stand
Before thy face and see
The glories of that heavenly land?
O Saviour, answer me

And bid my anxious fears begone.
Speak peace, and hope, and love,
And let me in thy way go on
Until I rest above.

For further reflection: Psalm 32:3–5

God's Mercies

Lord, thy tender mercies are
To our empty souls a gift.
They, our thoughts exceeding far,
Make our hearts to thee uplift.

Strip each one of filthy pride,
And take away our every care.
Let all our souls in thee confide,
And each one thy blessing share.

Make every conscience pure within.
Make every burden'd heart desire
A perfect freedom from all sin.
Let our thoughts to thee aspire.

'Tis to be more like thee, we pray,
To meekly walk with holy fear;
That we may live to thee each day
And keep thy Holy Spirit near.

Dwell near us, gracious Lord, we ask;
Keep us thy servants day and night.
May we perform with love our task
And always do the thing that's right.

Fearless, if thou but be our Friend,
If thou wilt tell us, we are thine.
Fearless, if thou wilt still attend
And faintly whisper, "thou art mine."

FOR FURTHER REFLECTION: LAMENTATIONS 3:22–25

Lines on the Death of Andrew Kead

Lord, has thy servant now gone home,
Never more to part from thee?
Hast thou said, My servant come,
Spend thine endless life with me?"

Has he ceased to labour here?
Has his crown to him been given?
Is he now no more to fear,
Safe at last with thee in heav'n?

His worn out body we have laid
In its silent resting place.
May it of his name be said,
"Left the earth to see thy face"?

Hast thou welcom'd his poor heart,
Call'd him from his toil away,
Given him of thy throne a part,
There to dwell with thee for aye?

Let him of that num'rous crowd
Sing thy gracious name always.
Let him loudest of the loud
Sing thine everlasting praise.

We hope to join him soon again,
To swell the song he sings to thee.
When we have done with earth and pain,
We'll help him through eternity.

For further reflection: 1 Thessalonians 4:13–14

Longing to Be Away

I long to soar away where bliss
Reigns majesty supreme;
Where there is nought but love and peace,
And Jesus is the theme;

Where in a bright immortal stream,
Thy beauteous image shines;
Where in that life-imparting beam,
Thy love the soul confines;

Caught up to dwell with thee above
Beyond a thought or care;
To drink forever of thy love
In yonder scene so fair.

'Tis for thine image that I long;
'Tis for that glorious day,
When I shall join the saints among
And leave this cumbrous clay;

That land where thou dost reign alone
In grandeur past my thought;
Where martyrs, prophets, all have gone,
Whom thou thyself hast bought.

The number waits some precious gems;
The throng is broken, not complete.
There yet are many diadems
In that holy place to meet.

For further reflection: Philippians 3:20—4:1

AND THEY CRIED,
THOU ART WORTHY

Hark! What bursts of holy love
Sweep along yon golden streets.
Listen to the joys above;
Fly, my soul, and taste its sweets.

O, the music's grander far
Than my longing soul can reach.
Jesus, let me join that choir,
And the music to me teach.

O my soul, my heart, my tongue,
Catch the words they're singing now.
As they sing around the throne,
Every heart and knee they bow.

Do not stray but drink it in,
Never from this view to roam.
Touch this tongue, let me begin
To help them, e'er I reach my home.

Come, celestial fire, descend,
Bring a living coal with thee;
Make this willing heart to spend
Itself in holy ecstasy.

Stay! Bright and holy vision stay;
Let me hear their voices still.
O, my soul, come fly away;
They need thy voice the song to fill.

FOR FURTHER REFLECTION: REVELATION 7:11–12

SORROW FOR SINNERS

Weep, my soul, o'er fallen man;
They know no peace below.
And what is worse, they never can,
When they from earth shall go.

In thickest gloom, their night will set
With no bright star to shine.
No ray of light will e'er be met
Throughout that dismal clime.

Then weep, my soul, that they should lose,
Thy fair abodes forego;
That for their portion, they should choose
The place of endless woe.

This thought with all its ponderous weight
Melts this poor heart with grief.
O mortals, strive before too late
That you may have relief.

O soul, thine own immortal life
Demands thy greatest care.
Speed quick'ning Spirit, end this strife,
Let them thy pity share.

Their eyes, they close against their peace
And strive to pass thee by,
And will not have thy great release;
Thy love and truth defy.

FOR FURTHER REFLECTION: ROMANS 9:1–5

IN THEE WILL I TRUST

O sacred name, thou art my trust;
I venture all on thee.
Let me not from thy love be thrust;
Reserve a place for me.

For all my hopes are now above,
Center'd in thy dear side.
Lord, it would melt a heart of stone,
The blood thy wounds supplied.

Cleft for me on yon Calvary's tree,
Thou most dear heav'nly Lamb;
Let all the world now flock to thee,
Be saved by thy great name.

For thou wilt never cast one out
That trusts to thy dear blood.
Thy word is pledg'd, and who can doubt
The everlasting God?

No, I can't doubt, but must believe
Thy sovereign pow'r to save.
Thy promise is thou wilt receive
All who for mercy crave;

Wilt welcome to thy bosom all,
Who trust thy gracious name;
And wilt not one, however small,
Put out at last to shame.

FOR FURTHER REFLECTION: JOHN 6:37–40

FULL OF SIN

Gracious God, thy love has shown
How full of sin I am;
And mourning my proud heart, I own
The victory to the Lamb.

By nature, I am black and vile
And cannot do thy will,
And by thy grace, I'm brought to feel
I should remain so still.

But now, thou'st taught me where to go;
I cannot stay away.
Help me then still, O Lord, to know;
Instruct me what to say.

I come to thy dear breath for grace;
O Lord, do take me in.
Teach me some note thyself to praise,
And wash me from my sin.

Lord, I am feeble, thou art strong;
Then keep me in thy sight.
Make me to guard against the wrong,
And do whate'er is right.

May pure and holy love be mine,
While I this valley tread.
And after death, Lord, call me thine;
In heav'n lift up my head.

FOR FURTHER REFLECTION: ROMANS 3:9–12

So Are My Ways Higher Than Your Ways

As far as heav'n is from the earth,
So far his ways exceed.
He spreads his love around our birth
And well supplies our need.

He speaks, and at his mighty voice
The elements stand awe'd.
He calls, the people of his choice
Hear his almighty word.

The dead revive, the deaf they hear,
The blind begin to see.
The name that makes them all to fear,
The same has saved me.

The voice that cried, "Awake from sleep!
Ye drowsy ones arise!"
The same has call'd me from the deep
And open'd these blind eyes.

His pow'r what sinner can withstand?
Who can refuse to come?
He speaks, 'tis done, from every land
His ransom'd ones return.

They own his pow'r, adore the love
That brought them to his face.
Their song is heard by those above,
The sweetest song of grace.

For further reflection: Isaiah 55:7–9

Doubts (I)

In gloomy night, when doubts prevail,
Watch, lest too strong they prove.
Haste thou to help me when I fail
Thy gracious name to love.

Thou know'st, O Lord, my anxious thought,
Lest I at last should stray;
Where not one glimpse of thee is caught
Throughout the endless day.

Lord, cast thy shield above my head
In every struggle here,
And when by Satan I am led,
Lord, be thou also near.

And take me from the tyrant's clutch,
Lest he complete my fall.
For 'tis for me and only such,
Thou camest for to call.

And when these gloomy doubts arise,
Be thou my sun to light
My feet along the path, my eyes
To gladden with the sight.

And make me thy dear face to see,
When sun and stars are gone.
Remember Lord, I fly to thee;
O let me cease to mourn.

For further reflection: Ephesians 6:13–18

THE JOYS ABOVE

Wake! O, my soul, hear thou the song
Of those redeem'd by blood.
Rise! Haste to mix that host among
To praise the Lamb of God.

In such a theme, stretch every nerve
His glories to make known.
Let every heart with pleasure move
While we his blessing own.

Lift up thy pow'rs to his great name;
Exalted let him be.
From every heart its honors claim
In true sincerity.

Dear Saviour, teach this heart to raise
Its highest honors here.
Help me to speak thine endless praise
In every mortal ear.

O, may the whole creation know
And thy great name adore.
Descend, O Sacred Spirit, now,
Teach me to love him more.

O, let me hear them e'er I go
To join in all their joys;
To hear seraphic spirits show
Thy praise with joyful noise.

FOR FURTHER REFLECTION: PHILIPPIANS 4:8

PRAISE: IN LOFTY STRAINS EXALT YOUR KING

In lofty strains, exalt your King,
In seraphic language, hail
To him the Lord; fresh honors bring.
Seraphs, angels, men prevail
To exalt this Lord of thine,
Who in glory is divine.

In holy raptures, let your soul
Raise his name above all else.
Make him of your thoughts the goal
And himself be all your wealth.
Let him be your heaven here,
His the only name that's dear.

In your songs, let him be prais'd,
And his glorious name be told.
Let highest strains on earth be rais'd,
And every mortal heart unfold
To receive our gracious God,
Dwell at last in his abode.

O, that some instructing guide
To my joyful heart may come,
To bid me spread his glories wide
Till I find myself at home.
There, I'll never cease to love
God with all his saints above.

FOR FURTHER REFLECTION: PSALM 148:1–5

SNARES

O, how many snares may we see
To trap the unwary and young.
Each set as best they can be
To lead to the thing that is wrong.

And if the young have not his grace,
How can they with Satan compete?
How shall they keep firm in the race
And guard against every deceit?

For all in this world, there is hope;
Only ask and he's promis'd to give.
His word, which himself he has spoke,
He has bid every sinner to live.

But the young have the world and its sin,
And a war in their members does rage.
A battle they have for to win,
And to help them the Lord will engage.

They have but to cry for his grace,
And this word he has left to invite:
"My children, come, seek ye my face
And with joy, I in turn will requite.

My son, do but give me thine heart,
Thy life shall then be beyond fear.
You shall have of my glory a part;
Thy name to my heart will be dear."

FOR FURTHER REFLECTION: PSALM 27:7—9

Snares.

O how many snares may we see
To trap the unwary and young
Each set as best they can be
To lead to the thing that is wrong
And if the young have not his grace
How can they with Satan compete
How shall they keep firm in the race
And guard against any deceit
Yet all tho' in this world there is hope
Only ask and he's promis'd to give
His word which himself he has spoke
He has bid any sinner to live
But the young have the world and its sin
And a war in their members does rage
A battle they have for to win
And to help them the Lord will engage
They have but to cry for his grace
And this word he has left to invite
My children come seek ye my face
And with joy I in turn will requite
My son do but give me thine heart
Thy life shall then be beyond fear
You shall have of my glory a part
Thy name to my heart will be dear.

AFTER JUDGMENT

Oh, but sinner, do you linger?
Stay you at the judgment throne?
Why did you not with your finger
Touch by faith the offer'd boon?
Tis too late now;
Justice now, not mercy's King.

"Can I not by explanation
Show the Judge my trying case?"
No, for it was your salvation
He desired you to embrace,
And you would not.
Now he offers you no grace.

Sinner, hear the thunders rolling;
See the chains, they come to bind.
Hear the flames disturb'd are roaring;
You're the victim they shall find.
For you trampled on the blood,
Dared a just and holy God.

You ask for mercy now, what for?
'Twas offer'd, but the gift you spurn'd.
And would you really now concur?
'Twas needful for you to have turn'd.
The day is pass'd forever now.
Why ask reprieve? Why tremble so?

But hark, they come, you're missing
From the number of the lost. They see thee
Haste. Why tarry from the retribution
Of your sins, and try to evade the fiery sea?
The books are clos'd
And now the key will turn and turn forever.

"But is there no escape from this?"
Oh no, the die is cast, and if 'tis ill,
Remember while in time the warnings did not cease;
Persuasion fail'd, and this, the evil,
Is but the penalty
Of unforgiven sin.

"Then if there is no hope, and I must go,
And through Eternity endure my lot,
Let this last word, that I have bought my woe,
Remain for those who like myself have blot
Their names out of the book of Life
To their eternal ruin.

And though this voice shall soon be hush'd in flames,
Yet still the justice of my sentence I will own.
And in the midst of darkness, his blest name
I'll praise in stifle'd sobs and groans.
For he in mercy linger'd lovingly,
Nor struck till death, enthrall'd me in the tomb.

FOR FURTHER REFLECTION: REVELATION 20:11–15

Doubts (II)

It's what I'd like to know,
For oft this heart distrusts:
Whether to heaven I e'er shall go,
Or from its joys be thrust.

Oft I'm perplex'd to find
Anything that's like heaven;
If anything of a heavenly kind
Is found in all my living.

But sometimes there's a joyous ray,
It seems of heavenly love.
But e'er I have it long, I say,
"Can it be from above?"

For all these changes seem to say
That it is all delusion.
A fancied spark of joy today,
Tomorrow in delusion.

But while I have such thoughts as these
And sink into despair,
Something still whispers, "There is ease
Where mortals know no care."

Then comes the thought, "But if I'm wrong
Where shall I find this treasure?
Or through eternity so long
Shall I enjoy this pleasure?"

But still this thought does comfort give,
There's promis'd strength to aid
The troubled minds; for while they live,
They by his strength are stay'd.

And when the heart fresh trouble feels,
And all things look so drear,
This balm has and will always heal;
In trouble he is near.

And in these darksome, lonely hours,
A light there seems to shine,
Which strengthens with fresh joy our pow'rs;
It seems a light divine.

Yet, still it's what I'd like to prove,
If I at last shall be
Taken away to dwell above,
To be at home with thee.

O, if this lot shall e'er be mine,
If I shall e'er be near
Thee, when in glory thou shalt shine,
Dear Jesus, tell me here.

I long, I pant, I wait to hear
Thy voice within this breast.
O come remove the cause of fear;
Jesus come, give me rest.

For further reflection: Romans 8:14–17

HEAVEN (II)

Yon beauteous heav'n, without one care,
Is freely given for us to share.
Then, will we sing as ne'er before;
We'll sing, and praise for evermore,

Express our thoughts in nobler praise,
And crown him King through endless days.
Then, will we talk of mercies past,
Of all his goodness first and last.

He caught us as we went astray
And led us in the narrow way.
He sav'd us by Almighty power
And kept us safe until this hour.

We'll walk the streets of heav'n with joy,
In praising, all our pow'rs employ,
In raising great hosannas to his name,
In speaking praises to the heav'nly Lamb.

We'll tell the wonders of his grace to us
Who died to save us from the curse,
And the arch'd vault of heav'n shall ring
While countless myriads praise their King.

There's no more sorrows, no more pains.
We'll sing in sweet melodious strains
And bid our harps resound the lays
That will not end in endless days.

Thus, will we spend that holy time
When nations come from every clime.
O, then our happiness will be complete
When all the blood bought race we meet,

Each member in his fitted place will be,
And all the triumphs over sin shall see.
Now saints on earth, when you such privilege have,
Look on this world, and when you're called to leave,

Gladly relinquish all for that dear place
Where sorrow, pain, and sickness, has no trace.
Remember, Christian, how that God has been
Your watchful Father, and to your welfare seen.

Think of his mercies, not of your distress
It must be for your good, or he would make them less.
'Tis all to make us fit to hold our place,
To bring fresh laurels to the heav'nly grace.

Then let us spend such holy happy days
And pray and labour on in heavenly ways.
If we but strive, the Lord will do the rest.
And then to urge us on in labour, we'll be blest.

Away with all our prejudice and pride;
Let's put aside the dark and view the brilliant side.
With patience, let us press the road that once was trod
By him whose name is Jesus and eternal God

For further reflection: Revelation 3:12

PRAYER: JESUS, O LET
THY PEOPLE HEAR

Jesus, O let thy people hear
Thy voice, though faint it be.
Let them but catch in accents clear
The words of life from thee.

Our everlasting Friend, come down;
Let us thy glory see.
And in thine own immortal bloom
Let all thy servants be.

Embrace us, Lord, before we part,
Bid every idol flee.
Bestow a fearing, loving heart
From sin that may be free.

In thy dear courts, we love to dwell,
Nor tired would we be
If thou wouldst come and say, "'Tis well,
I still remember thee."

Then in these peaceful joyous hours,
In raptures would we tell
The wonders of thy gracious powers
To save the soul from hell.

Dear Jesus, hear our plaintive cry;
We will not stay from thee.
Give but the wings of faith to fly
Across Eternity.

The distance seems so far away;
Thy throne we cannot see.
Rise, stretch thy wings, my soul, and say,
"Jesus, I fly to thee."

Jesus, we cannot stay so far,
So separated be.
Give us the faith, and with its pow'r,
We'll gain our liberty.

Earth cannot hold us here to dwell
In low humility.
Burst thou the bonds, and let us tell
The love we bear to thee.

More lofty strains than these we owe
To thee when we shall see.
And as eternal ages flow,
We'll still delighted be.

Help, O my Saviour, help this heart
To praise thee while I'm here.
Let heaven, and earth, and sea delight
To praise a name so dear.

A note above the songs of earth
Give me to praise thy name.
Exalted notes, angelic mirth,
Thy praises to proclaim.

FOR FURTHER REFLECTION: COLOSSIANS 3:1–4

Judgment Day

Sinner, hear yon dreadful sound
Pealing over all the earth.
Hark! The thunders, how they hound,
Scattering all the empty mirth.

See! This is the long'd for day;
Bright with all the heavens they shine,
Dark to those who've thrown away
Streams of mercy so divine.

The heavens, they rend and disappear;
The trumpet sounds more loud and shrill.
Hark! The summons, can you hear?
Louder, sadder, graver, still.

See the crowds prepare to flee;
Thus amaz'd, they wish to hide,
And the waves in seeming glee
Lashes in majestic pride.

See the earth's foundations broken,
Hear the pealing thunders roar.
Of the evil day the token
Tells of mercy that's no more.

Shrieks now meet on every hand;
More shrill, more awful still they grow.
But there's some who firmly stand,
Seeming danger not to know.

A voice invisible is heard,
Mustering far the dreadful scene,
And there issues forth a word,
"Now I come and come to reign."

Now the rocks and hills are riven,
Scatter'd flee on every hand.
This reveals the dead and living,
Gathering out of every land.

At this word, the sea affrighted
Yields the myriads from its waves;
Graves and hidden places lighted,
Nothing from this opening saves.

But the scene's not yet completed;
Hell delivers next her prey.
At the throne, in glory's lifted,
Sun and moon and stars decay.

The trumpet sounds in solemn stillness;
All this wondrous host stand awe'd.
And with penetrating clearness,
Voices echo, "Welcome, Lord."

Silence once again commands them,
And the host with mute surprise
Hear this theme again renewing,
"Jesus, King of Glory rise."

In solemn pomp, the Judge is seated.
Seraphs, angels, now rejoice.
For the Judge has called and greeted
All the people of his choice.

Angels bow, the ransom'd sing,
"Holy, holy, holy, Lord,
Thou art worthy mighty King,
Victory to th' eternal God.

Take immortal honors now,
Lo, our crowns and palms we give.
Here before thee now we bow,
And before thee we will live.

Thou art worthy to be prais'd
Through that long mysterious time.
To thee all voices shall be rais'd,
Thou hast brought from every clime."

"Welcome to your lasting rest;
You have fought and conquer'd now.
Welcome to my loving breast,
While eternal ages flow.

Angels, take the tares away.
Bind with everlasting chains
That throughout the ceaseless day
They may dwell in dying pains."

FOR FURTHER REFLECTION: REVELATION 11:17—18

PRAYER: TO THOSE OF ALL THE WORLD BEREFT

To those of all the world bereft,
Whose sorrows none but One can tell,
Whose cup is fill'd, whose asking breast
Refuse to think that all is well;
To those, who, stript of every joy,
Have none to pity, none to calm,
Be thou the sweet without the cloy,
Be thou their shield from future harm.

FOR FURTHER REFLECTION: JOB 1:18–21

Prayer: Awaken in My Soul a Pure Desire

Awaken in my soul a pure desire.
Come, Spirit, kindle some celestial fire
That shall dispel the gloom.

For what is life if thou art gone?
Where shall my soul then find a home
If thou but tak'st thy flight?

Come, Holy life-inspiring Dove,
Enliven, raise, uplift, remove
Whate'er thou seest wrong;

And hold me still to thy dear breast,
Fasten'd by chains, but not distress'd,
With chains of love like thine.

For further reflection: John 16:12—15

THE SINNER'S RESOLVE

I've a soul, I've a soul, and to save it I'll try,
And the king that I've served I'll desert.
To the crucified Saviour for refuge I'll fly,
Nor fear though they try me to hurt.

I am guilty, I am guilty, but what can I do?
To which of my acts can I flee?
My conscience upbraids, and tortures me so,
For no pardon at all can I see.

I've merits, I've merits, but they're not on my side,
And against me, I know they will turn.
For in thinking on works that were once all my pride,
With hot indignation I burn.

I've power, I've power, and this power I will prove.
For the works that I've done, I detest;
I will fly to the Saviour and ask for his love
And will trust to his word to be blest.

If he saves, if he saves, then what need I to fear?
For he says, "Come, ye needy and poor;
Come and eat, all ye hungry; ye thirsty, come near;
Come, for plenteous mercy's in store."

I will come, I will come and take it, dear Lord.
I will take thy free gift as a boon.
For if I don't come, I can hear from thy word,
Thrust forever from thee, I'll be soon.

O forbid it, forbid it, I come; Take me in,
Wash me thoroughly, make me quite pure,
Take away every stain, and forgive every sin,
And make my salvation secure.

I'm forgiven, I'm forgiven, I will bless thee for aye
And will count all my goodness but dross.
Only let me but sing of thy love all thy day
And nail all my sins to the cross.

I'm for heav'n, I'm for heav'n, nor can earth hold me now,
Nor can pleasures that earth can afford.
For my heart's fill'd with such a bright heavenly glow,
It is nought but thyself, my dear Lord.

I'm for joy, I'm for joy, and it's this I can find
That sin can no comfort impart.
The world with its pleasures I now leave behind,
And this gives me great comfort at heart.

I'm for glory, I'm for glory, for the glory that's here,
My soul must such tinsel despise.
'Tis not the true happiness my soul to cheer
That I'll have when I soar to the skies.

I'm for God, I'm for God, for 'tis he that can bless
And can cheer through eternity long.
'Tis he that will one day, his saints to him press
And cause them to sing the glad song.

FOR FURTHER REFLECTION: PHILIPPIANS 3:12—14

PRAYER: JESUS, MY LORD AND KING

Jesus, my Lord and King,
Engross my thoughts with thee.
Shew thyself, that my soul may cling
Alone, O Lord, to thee.

Speak from the highest height
Of thine eternal throne;
Be thou my soul's supreme delight
And make this heart thine own.

Prone to escape thy lov'd embrace,
And wander from thy love;
Prone to do despite to thy grace,
And lose the joys above.

Lord, if thou dost not still attend
Thy wand'ring child while here,
I shall prove worse, but never mend;
Be lost at last I fear.

But Lord, forbid the dreadful thought
That I at last should prove
A castaway whom thou hast bought,
A match for sovereign love.

Hear, Lord, I feel I must backslide
If thou thy strength withhold.
Come, dearest Jesus, safely guide
A wander'r to thy fold.

For if I should at last be lost
And should thy grace defy,
Th' accuser will be sure to boast
And raise his voice on high.

But Lord, the powers of heav'n and earth
Are given entire to thee.
O God, thou'st kept me since my birth;
Be merciful to me.

And when I'm safely with thee, Lord,
I'll tell in every ear,
The grace that sav'd me by thy word
Has kept, and brought me there.

And that's not all, for I'll declare
Thy goodness, and will show
That grace on earth that I did share
Would never let me go.

And through that long, long day, I'll sing
Thy praise, sweet, constant Friend,
And shout with all that praise their King,
And thus, the time shall spend.

Lost from thine hand, no I could not
Be lost when I am thine;
Thy word declares, without a spot
I shall in glory shine.

FOR FURTHER REFLECTION: 1 JOHN 5:10—13

DECEPTION IMPOSSIBLE

Swift as the eagle wings his lofty flight
Across yon azure sky;
Swifter by far, there shoots the light
Of God's all-seeing and unerring eye.

No deed of midnight darkness from his view can hide.
His penetrating eye ranges the earth around.
The eye of God has every secret spied,
Above the heavens and beneath the ground.

Has space a limit, that can ne'er unfold,
It holds no secret from his searching gaze.
Has earth a cavern that is yet untold,
It lies unmask'd before this awful blaze.

Is there beneath the vaulted arch of heaven
One who vainly tries to keep a secret dark,
Or in the blackest midnight that has striven
To deceive th' Eternal or elude his spark?

'Tis folly, madness, thus with him to act!
'Tis light as day the darkest seems to him;
No shadow can obscure each fact
Before whom present, past, and future gleam.

Ye might as well attempt to hide the sun,
Or bid each planet cease to roll on high,
Or make the earth his journey cease to run,
Or drag each planet, captive, from the sky.

Hear ye this word: the eyes of God are o'er
The heavens, the earth, the sea, and sky,
Observing each moment of the rich and poor
From his ethereal throne on high.

FOR FURTHER REFLECTION: JEREMIAH 23:23–24

129

PRAYER: SPIRIT OF LIFE, OF LOVE AND POW'R

Spirit of life, of love and pow'r,
Descend, and with a plenteous show'r
Bedew our every heart.
And let thine own redeem'd ones see
Thee, not in meek humility,
But glorious, as thou art.

Lord, e'er thy people leave this place,
Give but one glimpse of thy dear face
And prove that thou art here.
Then may thy people trust thee still,
Know and endure in love thy will,
And hold thy name more dear.

O, let us now thy glory see,
Gladden our hearts that we may be
Refresh'd and made more pure.
Give us a foretaste of thy love,
A sweet, enriching, hour above
The trials we endure.

FOR FURTHER REFLECTION: PSALM 85:4–7

161

GOD'S LOVE

Wonder, ye saints, that God so long forbears
To smite us with the rod, when most we need
Correction from his hand; yet still he looks
On us with pitying eye, and to the avenging angel turns
And says, "Forbear to strike; yet once again,
I'll try to bring the wanderers back."

Then with a voice of sovereign power and love,
He calls us by a voice that we well know,
And says, "Return, ye ransom'd of the Lord.
Did I thus bleed and shall I let you go?
Shall I my name and saving power give up?
For in an unguarded moment, you did step
Over to Satan's path, and he would fain have kept thee.
Have I not pledg'd my honor to preserve
And land you safely on eternal shores?
And shall I not my purpose carry out
And tread my foes eternally beneath my feet?
Then turn to me again with loud rejoicing heart,
And bid the powers of earth and hell defiance."

So bruise the head of him that bruis'd your heel
And say, "My Saviour conquer'd, and I will
Go on in strength the Lord vouchsafes to give
To those whose names are writ in heaven."

FOR FURTHER REFLECTION: HEBREWS 3:12—15

INVITATION

Oh sinner, if you could but see
Your Saviour as he prays to thee
To come and taste his love,
You'd fly into his lov'd embrace
And say, "Lord, give this heart a place
And let me serve thee here."

You'd love him, and you'd never part
With such a tender loving heart,
A heart that feels your woes
And promises to well supply
Your every need till in the sky,
You dwell among his choice.

Say, lost one, is not this enough?
A Friend when winds and waves are rough,
And storms shall howl around?
The Saviour offers you his love;
Grace more than angels have above
Is offer'd in this gift.

His hand shall guide your every day,
Shall keep you in the narrow way
And give you peace below.
His hand shall hold you when you're strong,
Shall place you in his glorious throng,
Shall bring you home to God.

For further reflection: Romans 10:8b–13

GOD'S COMMAND

Away, far above the ethereal sky,
There lives in grand abodes
Beings of stature very high,
Who guard the eternal roads.

In infinite space, they fly abroad
On errands from their King,
And ceaselessly they utter, Lord,
And songs of glory sing.

There sounds throughout the vast extent
A voice at which they bow;
And through creation, rocks are rent,
Mountains and hills lie low.

A summons issues from the throne,
A giant angel flies
Close to the throne and falling down,
Awaits the word to rise.

"Go tell the nations this decree;
Publish throughout the earth.
Vengeance is loos'd, and he will be
The end of all their mirth."

The guilt of generations come,
And cry for vengeance due;
The hosts of earth await their doom
And every sinner too.

Prepare, ye myriads of the tombs,
Tell why ye should not go
To where no hope, or mercy comes,
The place of endless woe.

FOR FURTHER REFLECTION: HEBREWS 10:30–31

Fear Not I Am with You

Why should I fear if he be near,
My Shepherd and my Guide?
Why flee before the foe or fear
If he be by my side?

O, let me in thy strength but trust,
Nor fear though hell oppose.
Of thy dear blood is all my boast
Until this life shall close.

If then we have thee near us now,
What may thy people dread,
When earth, and hell, and all below
Shall mingle with the dead?

O, let my voice but raise one song
When I arrive at home;
And this shall be the chorus long:
My victory's through the Lamb.

For further reflection: Isaiah 41:8–10

CALL TO THE SINNER

Return, oh foolish one, return!
Why wander from your peace?
Why all the warnings do you spurn,
And all your sins increase?

There yet is hope, if back you come;
There yet is room for all.
Why wander from your heavenly home
And spurn the heavenly call?

Return, return, ye long have stray'd,
Why longer still delay?
Why stands your soul condemn'd, dismay'd,
And yet you stay away?

Has reason fled, and left her throne?
Has love ceas'd from your breast?
Has reason left you to bemoan
The loss of heavenly rest?

Why tarry longer in despair?
Think of the blest reward.
Come, sinner, grasp this season fair
And close now with the Lord.

Thy heart is sad, but there is balm
To heal thy deepest woes.
The Lord shall keep thee safe from harm
And conquer all thy foes.

Close then with mercy while you're here;
Stay not another hour.
Lest you neglect this season fair
And never more have pow'r.

Remember, sinner, if you come,
'Twill save from every snare.
When death arrives, 'twill waft you home
The joys of heav'n to share.

Return then, sinner, pray return,
Lest having thus defied,
Throughout the endless time you burn,
O sinner, now decide.

<small>FOR FURTHER REFLECTION: 2 CORINTHIANS 6:1–2</small>

Christian's Thorny Road

See how yon Christian toils his weary way,
On each side dangers strew'd both thick and strong.
See you yon fiends are flitting in his path,
Now come, then for awhile retire,
Then again assembling with redoubled force.
They try, and sorely vex him,
And one more fiendish than the rest
Whispers in his ear some imprecation
That makes him start and tremble.

FOR FURTHER REFLECTION: 1 PETER 5:8—9

DELIVERANCE

A King look'd down on his domains
And saw the host were bound in chains.
Confusion like a giant strode
Throughout this people's vast abode.

And as he view'd awhile their state,
And mourning o'er their dismal fate,
This thought occur'd, "They might be sav'd;
A ransom got for the enslav'd."

This thought expanding fill'd his breast
With how they might attain to rest.
But with this thought his visage fell,
And why, e'en angels could not tell.

At length a counsel was conven'd
To hear what fill'd the royal mind.
'Twas this, that those now bound in chains
Might lose their yoke, escape their pains.

The kingdom dwelt in silence till he said,
"I've found a ransom, and the price I've paid
'Tis this that my own Son shall die
To raise these fallen creatures high.

He is the price that I demand.
He is the victim that shall stand
To loose them from the tyrant's yoke
And save them from th' impending stroke."

So saying, it was then agreed,
They from their bonds should all be freed.
And then at once it was resolv'd,
They from their sin should be absolv'd.

This met with acclamations long
And form'd the subject of their song.
'Twas this, the King divulg'd the plan,
While angels sang, "Goodwill to man!"

Time fled; At last, the time had come
When his eternal Son went down.
And as he went from heav'n to earth,
The choir of heav'n suspended mirth.

Some were dispatch'd of earth to tell,
This Son had come with men to dwell;
And this the reason why he came,
That men from sin he might reclaim.

No other price could e'er be paid.
No other victim e'er be had.
Our sins on Jesus Christ were laid,
While he our substitute was made.

He liv'd, he bow'd, at last he died;
In agony was crucified.
The price is paid, O doubt no more.
Sinners, your Saviour, now adore.

FOR FURTHER REFLECTION: PHILIPPIANS 2:6—8

On Hearing of an Infidel's Funeral

Here lies the last remains of that proud clay
That spoke against his God;
In blasphemy who spent his day
Now lies beneath the sod.

No more with boasting words he'll speak;
He lies now still and cold.
And that he took such pains to seek,
Before his eyes unfold.

In dreadful gloom and flames, he walks
And spreads his shrieks abroad.
No more of clearest proofs he talks,
He feels there is a God.

But mortal men, why risk his fate
And trample on the word?
Why spurn the gift until too late?
You seek a loving God.

Where can the puny soul of man
Expect to be at rest,
If not in glory, where he can
Forever there be blest?

Why should the helpless things call'd men
Uplift their puny arm
Against the ever blest Supreme,
Who speaks, and seas grow calm?

As well the fly determined be
To conquer man or die,
Or the small fishes of the sea
Defy the Lord Most High.

If but the slightest wish or breath
Be issue'd from his throne,
A wish would bring immediate death;
A bid, our souls be gone.

Who of the mightiest could bear
His glance of wrath to see?
A thought would send us far to share
Shame through eternity.

Then why rebel with such a foe?
Our safety is in peace.
And trembling at his feet lie low,
Let all our plea be grace.

For what can man expect to gain
By warring with his God?
There's nought but darkness, fire, and pain
Attending on his rod.

But though he's mighty, yet he loves
And made salvation free.
A cry for grace, his pity moves
And brings them liberty.

FOR FURTHER REFLECTION: PSALM 2:10–12

THE LORD OUR SHIELD

My heart is full, what can I say?
But he has led me all my way,
And he will keep me still.

And through the flowery paths he'll be
My faithful constant guide,
And by the pleasant streams he'll keep
Me safely by his side.

And when I roam among the hills
Of this uncertain way,
He will not let the lion seize
Or take me for his prey.

He'll keep me when I sleep and wake,
And when I go abroad.
He will not leave, nor yet forsake,
His pilgrim on the road.

And in the fight, he'll be my shield
And buckler by my side.
The sling and stone shall make them yield,
If he the strength provide.

And when the fight is all but done,
And foes are scatter'd far,
He'll bear me from the field with joy
And tend me by his care.

And when through fighting hard I faint
And look to him and pray,
His voice so sweet shall whisper, "Saint,
Thy strength is as thy day."

And when the last sad struggle's o'er,
And I've the river swum,
He'll meet me on the other shore,
Saying, "Welcome, welcome home!"

And when the pearly gates I see,
And entering by the door,
I'll know that I shall ever be
Praising for evermore.

Such heights of praise I then will give
To him that led me home,
Saying, "King Eternal ever live
With us around thy throne."

"Amen, amen," my soul will cry;
Eternity's too short
To sing thy praise; for years, I'll try
Nor do it as I ought.

But thou shalt teach us heavenly themes
And learn us music rare;
To praise thee we need heavenly hymns
With cherubim to share.

FOR FURTHER REFLECTION: PSALM 121:1–4

GUIDANCE

Lord, I am young and prone to stray,
Prone to depart from thee.
O, take this sinful heart away,
And make each sin to flee.

For though so young, I know I'm vile
And destitute of grace.
And none but thou can'st keep me while
I here prolong my race.

But in thine hand, my days are hid
And all my wand'rings here.
Let me in thee fore'er abide
And know no other fear.

And if thou should'st prolong my days,
I pray thee keep me still,
Learning, obeying all thy ways
And living out thy will.

Then what a joyful day t'will be
When thou shalt call me home;
Always thy glorious face to see
And never more to roam.

And through the hills in endless life
Where cherubs wing their flight,
Secure from every sin and strife,
I'll dwell within thy sight.

FOR FURTHER REFLECTION: PROVERBS 3:5—6

140

AND I WILL REMEMBER THEE FOR GOOD

Thou silent Watcher of the day,
Whose eye with penetrating force
Discerns each scene below,
Discern between the good and bad,
And mark each one for good that strives,
And let such meet with great success.
Those, who in singleness of heart and aim,
Desire to bring thy stray sheep to thy fold,
Enrich with every grace.

Let not a word be spoke in vain;
Let not an act whose object is to bring
Some wandering one to thee
Fall lifeless down.
Make all their efforts to produce thy will;
Send to them help, and make each day
Bring some new gems to deck thy crown.
These are our prayers, hear thou our sighs,
And answer them in peace.

FOR FURTHER REFLECTION: COLOSSIANS 4:2–6

AWAKE, O SOURCE OF HOLY JOY

Awake, O Source of holy joy,
Touch these cold hearts, these lips employ;
Teach me to strike my golden lyre,
Melt me, I wait, O sacred Fire.

FOR FURTHER REFLECTION: JOHN 15:4–5

I Am Thy Salvation

Salvation, speed and conquer all;
Bestow on all thy gracious boon.
Deliver nations from the fall,
And let them reign in glory soon.

The weary of the world and sin,
Oppress'd with guilt, a heavy load;
Bring, dearest Saviour, bring within
The weary's rest, the rest of God.

Salvation sweeps this earth from crime;
Let Eden once again appear.
Make earth as in her firstborn prime,
From sin, and death, and mis'ry clear.

Spread all thy peaceful charms again,
O thou, who mak'st the dead alive.
Scattering every sin and pain,
Lord bid the world again revive.

Make this long barren field rejoice
And bear the fruit that ne'er shall die.
Let those who here have heard thy voice,
Dying, into thy bosom fly.

Salvation, oh thou choicest ray,
Dawn to illumine earth's long night.
And on the wings of endless day,
Deluge the earth with holy light.

For further reflection: Acts 4:8–12

HINDRANCES

Ten thousand treacherous arts are used
To draw us from our God.
Satan has all his arts diffus'd
To stop the sacred word.

"I am the way," our Jesus cries,
And he must be our guide.
'Tis he that yields us our supplies
And all things right provides.

To fields of truth, he leads the way;
Truth is his life, his name.
And he reveals to those who stray
Away from him their shame.

In vain, deluded man may try
To search the world for truth.
The world the search will but defy
And leave us still to wrath.

In him alone, the truth does dwell,
And he reveals to all
Whose earnest cry and strong appeal
On Jesus' name shall call.

Pledg'd to attend the faintest cry
That men from earth can send,
He waits, and with a prompt reply,
Proves that he will attend.

FOR FURTHER REFLECTION: HEBREWS 12:1–2

ARISE, O GOD

Awake, thou arm, pledg'd for my guide;
When foes assail, be by my side.
Nor leave me to relentless foes,
Surrounded here by snares and woes.

Mighty in strength, thy conq'ring sword,
Draw, my defenseless head to guard.
Make them to flee before thine arm,
And let my anxious soul be calm.

Fear of thy foes, arise to show
Their near approach that I may know.
And with a word make them to fly,
When I shall breathe the faintest cry.

Surround me by thy shield, thy love;
Be near me too, when'er I move,
That all the host, and Satan's rage,
Lord, I may in thy strength engage.

O, leave me not; thy will shall be
Mine too, through time eternity.
And thy good pleasure I will bear,
Till leaving earth I lose each care.

And when the angel's trumpet's sound
Shall startle those beneath the ground,
Then may thy foes, and mine, array'd
With trembling hear their sentence read.

FOR FURTHER REFLECTION: PSALM 18:1—3

CONSCIENCE (II)

Thou gentle warning voice I hear;
Thy words of careful thought.
My friend who seest danger near,
When I myself see nought.

Thy anxious eyes see foes at hand
And gently whispers, "Stay"
And quietly warns to make a stand
Against each sinful way.

Shortsighted, I can see no harm
While nearing danger's brink.
But thou dost raise thy sure alarm,
"Before thou leapest, think!"

Thou watchful eye, be near me still,
And when my foes draw nigh,
Let me be govern'd by thy will
And from the danger fly.

When near the precipice I roam,
Let thy disturbing voice
Tell me I am away from home,
Far from my dearest choice.

Or when my foot forgets the road
And strays on ground not mine,
Lest I should get too far abroad,
Shew me the safest line.

FOR FURTHER REFLECTION: ISAIAH 30:19–21

Judgment (II)

O righteous Judge, before whose bar
The worlds assembled must appear;
Whose searching gaze no eye can meet,
Enthron'd upon thy judgment seat.

Thy righteous ire before the throng
Shall burn their wretched souls among,
And terrors seize them as they cry,
Forever thrust beneath the sky.

Is there a mortal, spurns thy love,
O thou the highest theme above?
Crimes, can there be one worse than this:
Refuse thy love, and spurn thy bliss?

O, could a mortal raise his hand
Against his Maker's just command?
Guilt of the deepest dye in space,
A worm rebel before thy face.

Where, though in worlds in space so high,
Is there a creature to defy
Thee, who in mercy hast prepar'd
A heav'n by mortals to be shar'd?

O, let these stubborn hearts desire
Thine offer'd grace, and to aspire
To where thine hand, hast made us homes.
O, be our Friend whose judgment comes.

For further reflection: Psalm 76:7—9

Heaven (III)

Beyond the glittering starry sphere,
There revels in the gorgeous light
Angelic forms both far and near,
Unceasing wing their lofty flight.

They bear the tidings to their King
That mortals own his gracious sway,
While heav'n with ecstasy does ring,
And Jesus bears the palm away.

But loftier still the notes ascend,
And tongues like thunder shake the plain,
And cherubim their voices lend,
Exalting Jesus who was slain.

Shouts beyond mortal ears to hear
Ascend from hearts redeem'd by thee,
And music, which 'tis but to hear
To live in holy ecstasy.

And myriads thronging at thy feet,
To hear thy welcome, see thy face,
And in immortal bursts to greet
A sound so sweet, thy sovereign grace.

Unheard the joys, unseen thy throne,
With ardent longing still we press
To be with thee, with thee alone,
The Lord of life, in happiness.

For further reflection: Revelation 5:11–12

CHRIST THE REFUGE

Christ is my refuge; all beside
Is nought compar'd with him.
When justice frowns, in him I hide,
And mercy shuts me in.

The law with all its thunders peal
Above my head in vain.
Safely from harm, I now can feel,
Jesus was for me slain.

And Satan with his poison'd dart
Can never make me fear.
Jesus his presence will impart
And keep my pathway clear.

Nothing shall harm the Lord's elect;
They stand secure and strong.
He will at once my foe detect
And guard me from the wrong.

Safely when all the clouds above
Are gather'd thick and dark,
Though in the valley, by his love
Safely I there shall walk.

Faithful, though I inconstant prove,
Near me with watchful eye,
Not for one moment will he move
Till to his arms I fly.

FOR FURTHER REFLECTION: COLOSSIANS 2:16–19

Prayer: By Nature
Left without a Ray

By nature, left without a ray
Of hope on which to rest,
One long, beclouded, darksome day
Fills every human breast.

And until thy bright star arise
To shed its light around,
In vain we dwell beneath the skies
Until thy light is found.

But when the beam from heav'n begins
To dawn upon our way,
Its sacred light in darkness springs
And turns our night to day.

Dawn, then, on those whose moral night
Calls loudly for thine aid.
Make darkness flee before thy light,
And let their shadows fade.

O, for a ray to pierce the gloom
And scatter clouds afar.
From heathen lands, and in their room,
Make them thy love to share.

Sweet beyond mortal tongue to speak
Are joys which here we feel.
Searching we find the pearl we seek,
And finding all is well.

For further reflection: Isaiah 60:1–3

ON PRAYER

My soul, stretch forth thy pow'rs to heav'n
And call the blessings down.
The answer shall in time be giv'n
Thine efforts here to crown.

Close by thee now, his ear attends
Who asks of thee to pray.
The same who all thy mercy sends
Is by thee night and day.

He waits thy pray'r; the answer now
Begins its sure descent.
His own right hand ere long will show
He hears thy sore complaint.

What! Leave the heirs of grace while here?
Refuse to hear their cry?
No never, saints, away your fear!
Your God can never lie.

His promise stands secure and fast,
His word remains the same.
He is our God, the First and Last,
The Lord our Strength, his name.

Wait, for some evil may betide,
Temptation, trap, or snare.
Thy pray'r is heard, he by thy side
Still guards thee, by his care.

FOR FURTHER REFLECTION: LUKE 18:1—8

FEAR NOT, FOR I
AM THY GOD

Though clouds and storms may rage below,
And gath'ring tempests sweep,
And trouble like a river flow,
And God appears to sleep;

Though mountains fall, and hills be mov'd,
And earth in tumult toss,
The people that he once has lov'd
Can never suffer loss.

He sleeps not, for his eye beholds
The various changes here.
His purposes he still unfolds,
While we both love and fear.

Beyond the present, future good
He brings from seeming ill.
He has in storms forever stood
To bid the waves be still.

And if the ages past have known
His mighty pow'r to save,
Will he leave us, no less his own,
Unheard, for help to crave?

Silence my heart, give hear my soul,
Remember still he loves.
His word, his oath, is pledg'd to call
Us up to where he lives.

FOR FURTHER REFLECTION: ROMANS 8:31–34

Prayer: O Lord, How Long a Week Appears

O Lord, how long a week appears
To be away from thee;
Beset with doubts, alarm'd by fears,
Without a pow'r [to] flee.

The world and sin surround my soul
With angry words and vile;
Assault and try to make me fall
With treachery and guile.

But from thy word, I draw supplies
Of grace to keep me true.
And as my num'rous foes arise,
They flee before it too.

Search, try this heart that it may love
No other gods but thee.
Beneath the sky or high above,
No other gods may be.

Nor gold, nor all this world affords,
Nor all its pleasures here,
Let them not draw me from thy words,
But keep thou me sincere.

And though so long away from thee,
Yet let me feel thy love.
And that I may thy glory see,
Learn me thy will above.

For further reflection: Psalm 84:10–12

SINS FORGIVEN (I)

O sweet the hour, O joyous day,
When sins so deep were wash'd away.
When I was told to fear no more,
And heard him say, I am the Door.

I am the Life, thy soul to me
Resign, that it may cleansed be.
Come, and thy wants I will supply
Till leaving earth, you soar on high.

Yes, Saviour, I'm resolv'd to come,
To find in thee my lasting home.
I tremble, yet I trust thy name;
I come. O, put me not to shame.

FOR FURTHER REFLECTION: PSALM 32:1–2

SINS FORGIVEN (II)

Now welcome sounds burst on my ear,
Acquitted through my Saviour dear,
Freed from the curse and brought within
His fold, away from care and sin.

Where from the mines of wealth can I
Obtain a gift to satisfy
Or to repay a debt so large?
By present, get a free discharge?

No, there is nought that I can give,
Nor can I pay it while I live.
It must remain, the debt I made,
A price that never can be paid.

FOR FURTHER REFLECTION: COLOSSIANS 2:13–15

155

CONQUERING LOVE

O ,Thou all-conquering Love can wield
The pow'r to break the heart;
Can make the stubborn will to yield
And soft'ning grace impart.

The stoutest heart must bend to thee
And own thy matchless sway.
Not hatred, sin, can armour be
To keep thy sword away.

O, let the love of Jesus crown
Our captive souls with peace.
For casting all objections down,
It bids our warfare cease.

And as beneath its pow'r we live,
Though conquer'd, yet no slave.
The world such freedom cannot give;
'Tis more than we could crave.

So sweet, so pleasant are its ways;
An hour eclipses far
The greatest joys, the brightest days;
With them cannot compare.

Its chains, not brazen links, but love;
Its fetters silken cords.
Such sweet constraint, 'tis like the dove,
Whispering its softest words.

FOR FURTHER REFLECTION: ROMANS 2:2—4

SABBATH (II)

Behold, the glorious Sabbath morn,
Its calm and peaceful rest.
A holy joy begins at dawn
To make us mortals blest.

Sweet time to leave our earthly cares
And meet the Sabbath's Lord;
Forget our trials, pass our snares,
To feast upon his word.

To see our purchas'd mansion there
Where nought of sin can be;
That land of joy, so wondrous fair,
A place prepar'd by thee.

Rejoice, ye wander'rs, to the home
Above in yonder height.
Wait until death's sweet voice shall come
And bid you take your flight.

Among the fields of endless peace,
Your weary spirits fly.
In holy joy which cannot cease,
Ye then shall rest on high.

Wait but a few brief moments here,
The Sabbath here begun
Shall usher in the Sabbath there,
When all the work is done.

FOR FURTHER REFLECTION: HEBREWS 10:24–25

Jesus All

Jesus, O sweetest name below;
None may with thee compare.
Thy name when first its force we know
Relieves from every care.

O, that the world, but knew thee now,
But knew thy priceless worth.
All men before thee here would bow
And gladly leave the earth.

One moment in thy presence here
Puts all the world in shade.
One moment now, when thou art near,
Makes all the world to fade.

Beauties so great we find in thee,
Beyond the mind to grasp.
Pleasures as boundless as the sea,
In thine embrace, we clasp.

Riches far more than stores of gold
Is ours when thou art seen.
Wealth more than mines shall e'er unfold
We find in thy dear name.

Honors surpassing kings, in thee,
Grandeur beyond our thought.
Yea all, and more than all we see,
Which thou for us hast bought.

For further reflection: Matthew 13:44—46

Jesus Christ the Same Yesterday, Today, and Forever

Jesus Christ, today and ever,
Still the same to mortals prove.
From us, dear to thee, to sever
Is to say thou wilt not love
Till the end of time the same.

But thy word is pledg'd to keep us
And present us at thy throne
Spotless, without blame, and fearless,
For to reign with thee alone
And to prove thy love the same.

Can we tremble, lest thy failing
Should involve thy precious word?
No, it cannot be; thy calling
Is forever when 'tis heard,
Always proving thee the same.

Can there be some foe withstand thee
That thy word shall lose its pow'r
Spoken? Art thou not almighty
To complete thine issue'd law?
O, then prove thy pow'r the same.

O, see ye mortals, he is near,
Hears thy cry and comes to save.
Know ye not? Ye need not fear.
You have but his help to crave,
And he'll prove his power the same.

For further reflection: Revelation 1:12–18

It Pleased God

It pleased God to bring me in,
To rescue me from all my sin,
To put his fear within my heart,
And all his graces to impart.

But far beyond a mortal's thought
Is why he should my soul have bought,
And why, when I in sin had stray'd,
On Christ should all my sins be laid.

But whence the spring, from whence the love?
Or what induced him to remove
The curse, the sin, my load of guilt?
What made his loving heart to melt?

Search all the world to find the cause.
Was it that we had kept his laws?
No 'twas not this; no cause we find.
It was in God himself confin'd.

Only it pleased him to buy
Rebels that they might dwell on high,
And to his name that he might raise
Peculiar people, to his praise.

O sovereign grace, election free,
This was the cause; he called me.
And I obey'd, because he drew,
And still sustain'd, he does that too.

For further reflection: Ephesians 1:3—6

Fear Not, It Is I

The storm gathers dark, but thine hand holds it tight.
Though thunders should roar, it will not me affright,
If I see thee beyond with thy glance toward me.
For thine hand holds the winds, and they cannot get free.

Should the waves of this troublous world overwhelm,
My soul, still be near me, and take thou the helm.
And the bark shall outride, e'en though heav'n should pass,
And in safety I'll dwell though creation should toss.

And amid all the myriads of spiritual foes,
Or when earth shall forget me, and friendship shall close,
Let me see thee beyond all the darkness. I'll sing
As I wade through the waters; to thee, Lord, I'll cling.

And when passing from all that below I hold dear,
On eternity's brink, be thou also near.
As I pass through the darkness, be thou, Lord, my guide
To instruct me to fathom the last rolling tide.

And when far from these scenes into space I shall fly,
Bid my soul wing its flight to the region of joy,
Where thou art in glory, transcendent, divine,
Beyond, where thy kingdom forever is mine.

And when on eternity's height I shall view
Thy myriads, and victory shall prove thou art true,
When all shall be thine and be rul'd by thy sway,
May I dwell beside thee on that glorious day.

FOR FURTHER REFLECTION: MATTHEW 14:24–27

161

VOLCANO (SECULAR)

In distant caverns of the dark abyss,
There rolls the liquid fire.
Then bursting with terrific hiss,
It spreads destruction dire.

Its mighty waves extending far,
In awful grandeur sweeps;
No limits can its progress bar
Till it, exhausted, sleeps.

Its belching, moaning, heaving mound
In agony is torn;
And spreading lower all around
Makes towns, and fields forlorn.

Ah grand, yet truly awful sight,
Thy molten stream descends,
Spreading its terrors with delight,
Nor stays to make amends.

Pompeii, thy tomb was form'd by this.
Thy sad, sad tale is known.
Thy glory in a moment's space
Entirely overthrown.

Upon thy ruins, still we track
The road destruction swept;
And memory calls the moment back
In which thy city slept.

FOR FURTHER REFLECTION: 2 PETER 3:10–13

Sickness

Why! Wasting sickness, art thou come?
Disease, why venture nigh
To take more victims to their home,
In fever graves to lie?

Wherefore art thou dispatch'd among
The creatures here below,
To track us in the busy throng
Or lay the needy low?

Why send the many ills to swell,
Through which poor mortals tread?
Are there not woes enough to tell
To lay us with the dead?

Then why to make these woes increase?
Dost thou appear to harm?
And suffer trouble ne'er to cease
By spreading thine alarm?

But if thou can'st not go away,
Commissions given thee here,
May I be ready any day
To meet thee without fear.

And if thou art employ'd to call
Us mortals out of time,
May I whenever I shall fall
Soar to yon healthful clime.

For further reflection: 2 Corinthians 12:7b—10

BLOOMING FLOWER

A flower there is that blooms
Within the breast of those
Who have escap'd the wicked's doom.
It springs, it buds, it grows.

A flower there is that blooms;
'Tis nourish'd with great care,
And tended it leaves little room
For wasting, dark despair.

This flower is of a kind
That's never seen by eyes,
But when its root ourselves we find,
It never, never dies.

'Tis nourish'd by some secret springs;
'Tis fed by food divine.
Its fruit is peace, which always brings
A lustre out to shine.

And in its leaves, there's healing balm,
And all its stem is love.
Religion is this flower's name,
And it is from above.

This is a flower that blooms
When all the rest are dead.
When they inhabit tombs,
This flower lifts up its head.

FOR FURTHER REFLECTION: MARK 12:28–31

Early Morn

Awake, ye chanters of the morn;
Tune your little pipes so shrill.
Bless your Maker at the dawn;
Do not keep your tongues so still.

Sing, ye merry little creatures;
Cheer the lab'rer at his toil.
With the sun's enlivening features,
Your melodious voice beguile.

Sing aloud, ye feather'd crew;
Nature smiles and God doth heed.
With the early dawn, do you
Fly from tree to tree with speed.

Wake the slumbering sleepy droves
With the echo of your notes;
Perch'd upon your lofty thrones
Let sweet music swell your throats.

Teach the nations, by your flight,
That beyond the starry sphere,
There is music to delight;
There are sounds more sweet to hear.

Let us learn of the contentment,
Smiles beneath a frowning sky,
And ne'er thinking of resentment,
Wait the will of God on high.

For further reflection: Matthew 6:25–27

REAPING

What's this sound I hear come sweeping
O'er the hills from yonder land?
Oh! It is the peasant's reaping,
Gath'ring in one joyous hand.

Hark! Again those sounds continue.
Sheaves are standing all around,
While they are working, heart and sinew,
Till with songs the harvest's crown'd.

See, the wagon's heavy laden;
With the smiling grain they're heap'd.
While each man and boy and maiden
Still are working, till 'tis reap'd.

Hear, they creak along the road;
Near the barn the wagons pull.
They with joy the sheaves unload,
Till the barn is stor'd quite full.

And now the last small sheaf is bourne [*sic*]
Into the barn and safely stor'd.
With thankful heart, they now own
The goodness of the harvest's Lord.

Thus, them that sow, with them that reap,
Rejoice together for success.
Though while sowing, they might weep,
With joy their sorrow God doth bless.

FOR FURTHER REFLECTION: MATTHEW 9:35–38

LOVE (I)

Come, where gentle breezes blow,
Fanning cheeks of roses.
Come, where neither cold nor snow,
But summers sun reposes.

Come, where leaves look fresh and green,
Where nature smiles with pleasure,
Where fruits and flowers may be seen,
Come there, my earthly treasure.

Why linger 'mid the blighting chills?
Speed you to yon dwelling,
Which nature with sweet fragrance fills,
And all around is smiling.

This clime's ill-suited for a weak
And tender plant like thee.
Stay not here, but let us seek
Some healthful clime to see.

I'll come and leave this with'ring soil,
No genial breezes blow.
I'll leave this place, where all is toil,
Away with thee to go.

I'll leave this sickly place behind
And dwell beneath the shades
Of orchards, for a home to find
Till life's last evening fades.

FOR FURTHER REFLECTION: EPHESIANS 5:25–30

PRAY, MURRAY

Written in a cooper's shop at dinner time while a cooper
was speaking against Christians and Christianity

Pray, Murray, hold there; do not be in a hurry.
Don't give your decision so fast,
For when people like you get into a flurry,
Their opinion is never the best.

You run down the Christians, they do you no harm,
And against you they would not offend.
Your words we don't fear, for they do not alarm.
Take advice then, your breath do not spend.

If to listen to you, we are now sitting here;
Little profit at last it will give.
When we want your advice, you won't give it, I fear;
So yours now we cannot receive.

You know that your words will not give any peace
Or pleasure, 'mid trouble and care.
Then I wonder you do not immediately cease,
And let's do what we like, which is fair.

I suppose you will die, like all other men here,
Then what will your boasting afford?
And when the last trumpet to wake you shall hear,
How then will you stand before God?

Are Christians the worst that you see all around,
That they your displeasure should have?
Stay! Your life is not one of the best, I'll be bound.
Look within, and some trouble you'll save.

FOR FURTHER REFLECTION: MATTHEW 12:35—37

LIGHT

Light, O how precious to our view!
Who art thou, welcome friend?
Thou every morn make'st nature new;
Thine help to all dost lend.

How precious art thou to the swain,
The rich, the poor; Thine aid
Is giv'n to all, that they may gain
Each day their daily bread.

But more than this, thou still dost bless
The earth, with plenty crown.
Light, but for thee, what deep distress!
How many here would mourn?

But for thine aid, our lot would be
A wilderness, a night;
Without a hope, or day to see,
A world without delight.

Thou slighted boon, so seldom blest,
I hail thy precious rays.
In golden hints, thou'st nature dress'd
And gilded weary days.

Then through the darkness, still I'll stretch
My eyes to catch thy dawn,
And wish for painter's art to sketch
Thee breaking into morn.

For further reflection: Matthew 5:43–45

CONTENTMENT

Beneath a burning sun we toil,
With care from morn till night.
And in one long continual broil,
We struggle or we fight.

On burning sands or winter's ice,
We mortals toil each day.
And all that we may but suffice
These wants that pass away.

On tinted fields, in busy throng,
We wander to and fro.
To heal some real or fancied wrong,
We make our blood to flow.

But why, for our short time while here,
Do we so urgent press
And shed full many a woeful tear
And make our comforts less?

There's woe enough beneath the sun,
And troubles all attend.
Ours it should be to join in one
These troubles to amend.

For why! 'tis but a sight, then past;
We leave these things below.
'Tis harder if we hold them fast,
At last to let them go.

FOR FURTHER REFLECTION: 1 JOHN 2:15–17

The Heart Speaking

Oh, why am I denied the bread
That others have and waste?
And why, while others thou hast fed,
Have I no food to taste?

Is such a course thy sovereign will?
While some abundance have,
Another mortal lacks his fill,
Compell'd the other's slave?

Or does the grasping hand of man
And cruel heart withhold
His brother's portion in his hand
And murders him for gold?

To heap up wealth, and let the poor
Be destitute, forlorn,
And make the human evils more
By causing them to mourn;

O Thou, who takest vengeance on
The wickedness below,
Remember those who bear the scorn
And suffer all this woe.

For what! that man may crush, to gain
The sordid dust while here.
To thee we cry, O see the pain
That mortals have to bear.

For further reflection: James 5:1—6

SUMMER

With golden rays, thy days pass by;
For nature seems to like thee best,
Bestows on thee a rich supply,
And entertains thee like a guest.

For scarcely has thy morn appear'd,
And spring's first efforts swept away
The last of winter, and has clear'd
A pathway for thy beauteous ray;

When nature spreads her plenty round
And calls forth birds on bush and tree,
Bestows her beauties on the ground
To usher in thy morn with glee;

And as thy first approach we know
And see by tokens thou art near,
E're we can think, thy beauties flow
And place before us of thy cheer.

But when arriv'd and at thine height,
Who can e'en estimate thy worth?
Thy happy days, so sweetly bright,
Inspiring all with joy and mirth.

But transient thou art, passing on
To visit others with thy beams.
Here but awhile, then past and gone,
We yet retain thee in our dreams.

FOR FURTHER REFLECTION: ECCLESIASTES 11:7—8A

DEATH

Swift as the lucid meteor cut the air,
So swift is death, and swifter far.
He flies with summons over sea and land
And deals his blows on every hand.

Sure as his errand, so his blow he gives;
After his stroke, no mortal ever lives.
There fall before him all beneath the sky;
The beggar, princes, kings before him die.

With piercing dart, he strikes, and mortals fall.
He heeds not cries, however loud they call.
The moment come, he waits not for a breath;
He seals the peasant, king, and prince in death.

He knows no mercy, heeds not any voice.
He walks in stillness, strikes amid the noise.
The battlefield, the cottage of the poor,
The lordly hall, he passes not a door.

Tumult and peace, alike will give him work
In broadest daylight, or in stillness dark.
He flies from pole to pole, until his work shall cease
In scenes of bloodshed, or in tranquil peace.

His hand o'ertakes in midst of worldly pride,
On mountains, hills, or on the silvery tide.
A moment here, he comes, we pass away
To dreadful darkness, or to cloudless day.

FOR FURTHER REFLECTION: PSALM 90:3—6

SONG: TELL ME
SWEET SONGSTER

Tell me sweet songster, who thou art?
For whose praise dost thou sing?
In what bright choir tak'st thou a part,
Thou lovely little thing?

Art thou now warbling out his praise,
Who form'd thee by his word,
And trying some faint note to raise
To thy Creator God?

If that's thy task, continue still
To warble out thy lays,
And with thy music, meadows fill
With thy Creator's praise.

If from so small a tongue as thine
His praise can be proclaim'd,
Why should I hold this tongue of mine
For praising that was fram'd?

For thou would'st put this face to shame,
If I should silent be.
And never magnify the name
That is so good to me.

No, I cannot hold my tongue
And silent keep this heart,
Until his praises I have sung
And with thee, bourne [*sic*] my part.

Then start again and let me try
To swell thy song of praise
And when thou sing'st again on high
Let me repeat thy lays.

For further reflection: Psalm 84:1—4

Song: Peep Again, O Sun

Peep again, O sun, shine through the drops of rain,
With us but a season to remain.
Scatter each dull, o'erhanging cloud,
And cheer the pilgrim on the road.

Shine to cheer the dull and weary;
Do not always be so dreary.
Let thy bright enlivening rays
Cheer us through the summer days.

Shine to gild the hours of toil
And to nourish nature's soil.
Help the sower and the seed
Both to health and plenty lead.

Let thy beams delight our mind
For in thee we pleasure find,
That our task we may go through
As we see that thou dost do.

Let thy healthful beams arise;
Scatter darkness from our eyes.
Pierce the veil that hides thy face,
With thy light the darkness chase.

For further reflection: Jeremiah 31:35—36

LOVE (II)

O Love, thy sweet'ning influence shed
Through all my mind and will.
Let nothing in this bosom tread
Unless it love fulfill.

Let love's entrancing arms bestow
On this distracted heart
A calm, and peaceful, heavenly glow,
And ecstasy impart.

Spread through the actions of my life
Thy soft and gentle hand.
In every trial, every strife,
Take thou the chief command.

For blest with thee, each day shall shine,
Each moment glow with peace.
From youth until my days decline,
Ne'er make this love to cease.

And always let its beam arise
When all things round are dark.
Let fall before my longing eyes
Its tiny sacred spark.

Gilding and sweet'ning every ill
And making troubles melt,
That it with joys my heart may fill,
The joys that may be felt.

FOR FURTHER REFLECTION: ROMANS 5:1–5

BURIAL GROUND

Mortals! Tread soft, 'tis holy ground.
Beneath this lovely sod,
Myriads now lie in sleep profound,
Who on this earth once trod.

They sleep, and yon bright moon shines on
The slumbers of the dead.
In solemn silence, we may roam,
This hallow'd portion tread.

Here rests the weary from his toil,
The master with the slave;
Together lie in native soil
All equal in the grave.

The guiltless with the guilty lie,
Until the morning dawn,
When silver trumpets loudest cry
Shall wake some up to mourn.

But they to whom the Lord has spoke,
To whom salvation's given,
Shall rise, and wrapt in Jesus' cloak,
Shall pass away to heaven.

Ah! Mournful sight, yet favour'd home
Of all the weary here.
May I when thy sweet rest shall come
Depart without a tear.

FOR FURTHER REFLECTION: 1 CORINTHIANS 15:51—55

FRIENDSHIP

Is anything beneath the sun
More welcome than a friend?
A heart in life that has begun
With other hearts to blend?

If there's a sight beneath the sky
Would make this heart to glow,
'Tis this, that one whose rank is high
Humility should know.

Who'd leave the gilded mansion's door
To bring the outcasts in;
A rich man caring for the poor
And lifting them from sin.

Whose heart would feel another's woes.
Whose sympathies extend,
Some painful, smarting, wound to close,
'Tis such a one's a Friend.

There's friends of divers sorts about,
But few who e'er intend
To help the poor and carry out
The meaning of a Friend.

A word, a hand, we need it all;
True friendship should be near.
In danger, and without a call
Should prove themselves sincere.

FOR FURTHER REFLECTION: JOHN 15:12–16

RICHES

A car stood at a rich man's door
With costly trappings hung.
Within he sits, forgets the poor;
His fellow mortals wrong.

His riches are of vast extent;
His servants homage pay;
He never thinks they are but sent
To him but for a day.

"My hand hath all this treasure got!"
The pompous worldling cries.
Nay stop, there is but one small spot
Where every mortal lies.

This is not thine, 'tis but thy trust;
To use it well take care.
Remember thou art only dust,
The hungry need a share.

The lame, the halt, the sick, the blind
Are sent for thee to feed.
The stranger and the weak in mind,
Rich man, supply their need.

Riches without a feeling heart
Are but a curse to man.
A cheerful giver takes a part
And gives whate'er he can.

FOR FURTHER REFLECTION: LUKE 14:12–14

THE ROSE

True emblem of a broken heart:
A rose with drooping head.
One hour in health and bloom thou art,
Another lying dead.

Some accident perchance hath laid
Thy lovely colours low,
And in a moment made thee fade
And made thine head to bow.

Ah! Common fate; some brutish hand,
Even to mortals, strikes the deadly blow.
And men as flow'rs, fall at death's command,
Cover'd with fading leaves, or driven snow.

FOR FURTHER REFLECTION: PSALM 103:15—18

VANITY

Leave all thy gaieties fair maid,
Nor squander all thy days.
Beauty shall like a blossom fade
Or pass like sunbeam's rays.

Leave all this tinsel, glitter, show;
These transient pleasures, spurn.
A higher source of joy to know,
A richer source to learn.

FOR FURTHER REFLECTION: 1 PETER 3:3—6

LOVE (III)

Love, 'tis a barren heart that never moves to thee;
A rock of adamantine sort that can defy thy power.
Touch'd by thy dart, we captive mortals see
A rose, a lily, or a violet flower.

FOR FURTHER REFLECTION: 1 CORINTHIANS 13:13

O Aeolus Lyre

Sweet music such as heaven alone can make
Wells up from thee, Aeolus' lyre;
While all our pow'rs thou dost captive take,
Blow, gentle breeze, and set this soul on fire.

FOR FURTHER REFLECTION: JOHN 3:8

Reason

Reason, thou precious gift, some lack thee
Whose clouded brain is restless as the sea;
Shut out from earth's best treasure, wander forlorn
Across this desert earth fore'er to mourn.

FOR FURTHER REFLECTION: PROVERBS 1:7

SUN

O glorious orb, why hide thy face?
Stay, let thy beams still shine.
Sink not so soon; yet stay apace,
Thou gift so much divine.

FOR FURTHER REFLECTION: PSALM 19:4—5

MUSIC

Insensible to be by music now
Is to have lost one's soul;
The sweet, enchanting pleasures run
Through every chord, both rise and fall.

FOR FURTHER REFLECTION: PSALM 33:2—3

BLISS

Seize, O my mind, this happy hour;
Let it not vanish, yes, 'tis gone.
Yet still remembrance shall with all its power
Reflect its brightness, as it passing, shone.

<small>FOR FURTHER REFLECTION: PSALM 77:11</small>

The Published Poems &
Hymns of C. H. Spurgeon

FALL OF JERICHO[†]

Cambridge / Waterbeach, 1852

The day is come, the seventh morn
Is usher'd in with blast of horn,
Tremble, ye tow'rs of giant height,
This is the day of Israel's might.
Six days ye mock'd the silent band,
This hour their shout shall shake your land.
Old Jordan's floods shall hear the sound,
Yon circling hills with fear shall bound.

Thou palm-tree'd city, at thy gates
Death in grim form this moment waits;
See, hurrying on the howling blast,
That dreaded hour, thy last, thy last.

Lo, at the leader's well-known sign
The tribes their mighty voices join,
With thund'ring noise the heavens are rent,
Down falls the crumbling battlement;
Straight to the prey each soldier goes,
The sword devours his helpless foes.
Now, impious! on your idols call;
Prostrate at Baal's altar fall.
In vain your rampart and your pride,
Which once, Jehovah's power defied.

Now Israel, spare not, strike the blade
In heart of man, and breast of maid;
Spare not the old, nor young, nor gay,
Spare not, for Justice bids you slay.

[†] *S&T* 1865:27. See also *Autobiography* 1:219.

225

Who shall describe that dreadful cry?
These ears shall hear it till they die.
Pale terror shrieks her hideous note,
War bellows from his brazen throat,
Death tears his prey with many a groan,
Nor earth itself restrains a moan.

Ho! vultures to the banquet, haste,
Here ye may feast, and glut your taste;
Ho! monsters of the gloomy wood,
Here cool your tongues in seas of blood.

But no; the flames demand the whole,
In blazing sheets they upward roll;
They fire the heavens, and cast their light
Where Gibeon pales with sad affright;
A lurid glare o'er earth is cast,
The nations stand, with dread aghast.
The shepherd on the distant plain
Thinks of old Sodom's fiery rain;
He flies a sheltering hill to find,
Nor casts one lingering look behind.
The magian scans his mystic lore,
Foretells the curse on Egypt's shore;
The Arab checks his frighted horse,
Bends his wild knee, and turns his course.
E'en seas remote behold the glare,
And hardy sailors raise their prayer.

Now, in dim smoke, the flames expire
That lit the city's fun'ral fire,
The glowing embers cease to burn:
Haste, patriot, fill the golden urn!
In crystal tears her dust embalm,
In distant lands, in strife or calm,

Still press the relic to thy heart,
And in the rapture lose the smart!

It must not be; her sons are dead,
They with their mother burned or bled;
Not one survives: the vip'rish race
Have perish'd with their lodging-place.
No more lascivious maidens dance,
No youths with lustful step advance,
No drunkard's bowl, no rite unclean,
No idol mysteries are seen.
A warrior stands in martial state,
And thus proclaims her changeless fate:
"Accursed city, blot her name
From mind of man, from lip of fame.
Curs'd be the mail, and curs'd his race,
Who dares his house on thee to place;
He founds it on his firstborn's tomb,
And crowns it with the brother's doom."

Thus God rewards the haughty foe,
Great in their sin and overthrow.
He ever reigns immortal King;
With Israel's song the mountains ring.

Yet 'mid the justice dread, severe,
Where pity sheds no silv'ry tear,
A gleam of golden mercy strays,
And lights the scene with pleasing rays.

One house escapes, by faith secure,
The scarlet thread a token sure,
Rahab, whose seed in future time
Should bear the virgin's Son sublime.

Thus, when the Thund'rer grasps His arms,
And fills our earth with just alarms,
His hand still shields the chosen race,
And 'midst his wrath remembers grace.

FOR FURTHER REFLECTION: HEBREWS 11:30—31

THE ONE REQUEST[†]

Cambridge / Waterbeach, June 1853

If to my God I now may speak,
And make one short request;
If but one favor I might seek
Which I esteem the best, —

I would not choose this earth's poor wealth;
How soon it melts away!
I would not seek continued health;
A mortal must decay.

I would not crave a mighty name;
Fame is but empty breath.
Nor would I urge a royal claim;
For monarchs bow to death.

I would not beg for sinful sweets;
Such pleasures end in pain.
Nor should I ask fair learning's seats;
Love absent, these are vain.

My God, my heart would choose with joy,
Thy grace, Thy love, to share;
This is the sweet which cannot cloy,
And this my portion fair.

FOR FURTHER REFLECTION: PSALM 16:5—8

[†] *Autobiography* 1:293.

IMMANUEL[†]

Cambridge / Waterbeach, June 1853

When once I mourned a load of sin,
When conscience felt a wound within,
When all my works were thrown away,
When on my knees I knelt to pray,
Then, blissful hour, remembered well,
I learned Thy love, Immanuel!

When storms of sorrow toss my soul,
When waves of care around me roll,
When comforts sink, when joys shall flee,
When hopeless gulfs shall gape for me,
One word the tempest's rage shall quell,
That word, Thy name, Immanuel!

When for the truth I suffer shame,
When foes pour scandal on my name,
When cruel taunts and jeers abound,
When "bulls of Bashan" gird me round,
Secure within my tower I'll dwell,
That tower, Thy grace, Immanuel!

When hell, enraged, lifts up her roar,
When Satan stops my path before,
When fiends rejoice, and wait my end,
When legion'd hosts their arrows send,
Fear not, my soul, but hurl at hell
Thy battle-cry, Immanuel!

[†] *Autobiography* 1:294; *SOOH* 13.

When down the hill of life I go,
When o'er my feet death's waters flow,
When in the deep'ning flood I sink,
When friends stand weeping on the brink,
I'll mingle with my last farewell,
Thy lovely name, Immanuel!

When tears are banished from mine eye,
When fairer worlds than these are nigh,
When Heaven shall fill my ravish'd sight,
When I shall bathe in sweet delight,
One joy all joys shall far excel,
To see Thy face, Immanuel!

FOR FURTHER REFLECTION: MATTHEW 1:21–23

THE NOBLE ARMY
OF MARTYRS[†]

Cambridge, December 1853

Rouse thee, Music! Rouse thee, Song!
Noble themes await thee long.
Not the warrior's thund'ring car,
Not the battle heard afar,
Not the garment rolled in blood,
Not the river's redden'd flood;
Subjects more sublime I sing,
Soar thee, then, on highest wing!

Sing the white-robed hosts on high,
Who in splendor suns outvie;
Sing of them, the martyr'd band,
With the palm-branch in their hand:
Fairest of the sons of light,
Midst the bright ones doubly bright.

Who are these? Of noble birth?
Were they monarchs of the earth?
Kings of Babel's ancient state,
Lords of Persia, proud and great,
Grecian heroes, bold and brave,
Romans, making earth their slave?

No,—but hearken! Heav'n replies,
List the music from the skies: —
"These are they who dared to die,
Champions of our Lord on high.
At His name they bow'd the knee,
Sworn to worship none but He.

[†] *Autobiography* 1:300.

Fearless of the tyrant's frown,
Mindful of the promised crown;
Trampling on Satanic rage,
Conqu'ring still from age to age.
Come, the glorious host review,
March the glittering squadrons through."

Some, from show'rs of deadly stones,
Some, from wheels, — with broken bones,
Snatch'd by sweet seraphic might,
Borne above the tyrant's spite, —
Wondrous in their dying hour,
Rose above the demon's power.

Some by cruel racks were torn,
Others were in sunder sawn.
Hunger, nakedness, and thirst,
Sword, and axe, and spear accurs'd,
Cross, and knife, and fiery dart,
All conspiring, join'd their smart;
Yet, unconquer'd e'en in death,
Triumph fill'd their latest breath.

Yonder rank in chariots came,
Blazing o'er with fiery flame;
Now, in burnish'd arms they shine,
Glorious in the gift Divine.

Some, from jaws of cruel beasts,
Rose to Heav'n's triumphal feasts;
Some, in dungeons long immured,
Saw in death their crown secured,
Writhing in their tortures dread,
Smiled as if on downy bed.

These, from Rome's dark dungeons flew;
These, on Alps, the despot slew;
These, by Spanish priests were slain;
These, the Moslem curs'd in vain.

Yonder stands a gallant host,
Martyrs from the Gallic coast,
Heroes from Bartholomew,
Soldiers to their Master true.

These, again, in shining row,
Saw the fiery torments glow,
They in Smithfield kiss'd the stake,
Blest to die for Jesus' sake.

Those who, further in the plain,
Lift to Heav'n the lofty strain,
In the ocean found a grave,
Plung'd by force beneath the wave.

Some by English prelates tried,
On the scaffold firmly died;
Scorn'd to own prelatic sway,
Nobly dared to disobey.

Covenanters bold are there,
Sons of Scotia's mountains bare,
Mingled with the valiant band,
Heroes of my fatherland.

FOR FURTHER REFLECTION: HEBREWS 11:36—40

MARRIED LOVE[†]

Hull, September 1865

Over the space which parts us, my wife,
I'll cast me a bridge of song,
Our hearts shall meet, O joy of my life,
On its arch unseen but strong.

E'en as the stream forgets not the sea,
But hastes to the ocean's breast,
My constant soul flows onward to thee
And finds in thy love its rest.

The swallows must plume their wings to greet
New summers in lands afar;
But dwelling at home with thee I meet
No winter my year to mar.

The wooer his new love's name may wear
Engraved on a precious stone;
But in my heart thine image I wear,
That heart has been long thine own.

The glowing colours on surface laid,
Wash out in a shower of rain,
Thou need'st not be of rivers afraid,
For my love is dyed ingrain.

[†] *S&T* 1865:460. For a facsimile of the original, handwritten poem, see *Autobiography* 2:298–99.

And as ev'ry drop of Garda's lake
Is tinged with the sapphire's blue;
So all the powers of my mind partake
Of joy at the thought of you.

The glittering dewdrops of dawning love
Exhale as the day grows old,
And fondness, taking the wings of a dove,
Is gone like a tale of old.

But mine for thee from the chambers of joy,
With strength came forth as the sun,
Nor life nor death shall its force destroy,
For ever its course shall run.

All earthborn love must sleep in the grave,
To its native dust return;
What God hath kindled shall death outbrave
And in heav'n itself shall burn.

Beyond and above the wedlock tie
Our union to Christ we feel,
Uniting bonds which were made on high
Shall hold us when earth shall reel.

Though he who chose us all worlds before,
Must *reign* in our hearts alone,
We fondly believe that we shall adore,
Together before his throne.

FOR FURTHER REFLECTION: SONG OF SONGS 8:6—7

POPERY[†]

Ye Protestants of England
Bestir yourselves to prayer,
Go search the Scriptures, and you'll find
The *true* religion there.

No orders, unction, penance, mass,
For sin can e'er atone,
But faith in the Redeemer's blood,
And faith in that alone.

No priestly witchcraft can absolve
A sin however small,
But to the Saviour we must go,
His blood can cleanse from all.

How weak to think that paltry gold
Can stay this fleeting breath,
Or that a touch of holy oil
Can save from second death.

Our creed requires not any man
To live a single life,
But he may love and cherish well,
That precious gift, a wife.

The Scripture tells us that Jesus reigns,
And reigns supreme alone,
No virgin saints or idol god
May vault into his throne.

Will English freedom, Englishmen,
Be ruled by a Popish word?
Shall England's civil rights be sway'd
By Rome's proud Papal lord?

_____

[†] *S&T* 1866:186.

Let superstition dark and vain
Be banish'd from *our* home,
And those who will such folly have,
Go search for it at *Rome*.

My fellow-countrymen, arise,
List to the Saviour's call,
Beware of empty sophistry,
Make Christ your all in all.

FOR FURTHER REFLECTIONS: COLOSSIANS 2:6–10

THE DROPPING WELL
OF KNARESBOROUGH[†]

Though this well hath virtues rare,
And excites a just surprise;
There is yet a well more fair
And more wondrous in mine eyes.

Blessed well on Calvary's mount,
Where the side of Jesus slain,
Mercy's own peculiar fount,
Pours a *stone-removing* rain.

See the heavenly blood-drops fall
On a heart as stern as steel;
Though 'twas hard and stony all,
Lo, it now begins to feel.

Legal hammers failed to break,
Flames of wrath could not dissolve,
None the stolid soul could shake,
Fixed in fatal firm resolve.

But the blood performs the deed,
Softens all the heart of stone,
Makes the rock itself to bleed,
Bleed for him who bled t'atone.

[†] *S&T* 1866:293. The water in the dropping well of Knaresborough, North Yorkshire, flows over limestone and is highly calcified, so that it petrifies anything that is placed beneath in the well.

As the crimson shower descends
All the stone is washed away;
Stubbornness in sorrow ends,
And rebellious powers obey.

Hewn from out the pit of hell,
And in Calvary's fountain laid;
By that sacred dropping-well
Be my soul more tender made.

Till my heart contains no more
Of the stone by which it fell,
But on Canaan's happy shore
Sings the sacred dropping-well.

FOR FURTHER REFLECTION: EZEKIEL 36:24–27

THE REFINER'S FIRE[†]

No sorrowful cross
Of sickness or loss,
Has in itself virtue to purge away dross.

One furnace alone,
With breath of grace blown,
Can soften and hallow this heart of a stone.

With delicate skill,
And fuel at will,
The Savior refineth and purgeth us still.

His love never tires,
But kindles new fires,
To burn up our idols and paltry desires.

The dross that will stay
In flames of to-day,
More fuel tomorrow shall melt it away.

As fresh scums arise,
Fresh faggots he tries,
And ever keeps melting, and thus purifies.

[†] *S&T* 1877:223. This poem was originally composed by John Berridge (1716–93). Spurgeon made edits to the third, fifth, eighth, and ninth verses.

Where flesh can't survive
Grace gets a revive,
And in a bush burning will crackle and thrive.

Thine heavenly art,
Great Chemist, impart,
To separate tinsel and dross from my heart.

And let me not dread
The furnace to tread,
But conquer the world through Jesus my Head.

FOR FURTHER REFLECTION: MALACHI 3:2—3

ALL GLORY[†]

We saints rejoice to lift our voice
With "glory, glory, glory,"
And loudly raise our songs of praise
To thee, O King of glory!

While warbling notes from tiny throats
Trill glory, glory, glory,
Our human words shall join the birds
With glory, glory, glory;

Thou, God of love, who dwell'st above
In glory, glory, glory,
Our souls inspire with heavenly fire
To sing alone thy glory.

The gorgeous flowers in leafy bowers
Blaze glory, glory, glory
While odours sweet, their Lord to greet,
Breathe glory, glory, glory;

The forest-trees with every breeze
Lisp glory, glory, glory;
And God-made dyes paint sunset skies
With glory, glory, glory;

The orchards' glow, the glistening snow
Beam glory, glory, glory,
And ocean foam and azure dome
Tell out the tale of glory.

[†] *S&T* 1882:17. This poem was written by Spurgeon after reading a poem published by his son, Thomas, also entitled "All Glory." Thomas's poem can be found in *S&T* 1881:619.

The babbling brooks in rocky nooks
Splash glory, glory, glory,
And silver streams and sunniest beams
Shine glory, glory, glory;

Sun, moon, and star on high afar
Gleam glory, glory, glory,
And waving corn the fields adorn
With glory, glory, glory,

And hill and dale, and mountain vale,
And rainbow arch of glory,
And moss and shell by beach and dell
All speak their Maker's glory.

O Lord, we pray, accept our lay
Of glory, glory, glory,
While journeying here to yonder sphere
Of glory, glory, glory;

Let toil nor dust impair our trust
Of glory, glory, glory,
Defile our walk, or soil our talk
Of glory, glory, glory;

But free from shame, be praised thy name
From youth till hairs are hoary,
And thee we meet for converse sweet
In glory, glory, glory.

FOR FURTHER REFLECTION: PSALM 29:1–2

A War-Song
or
A Battle Hymn†

Sung at The Pastors' College Conference 1885

Forth to the battle rides our King,
He climbs his conquering car;
He fits his arrows to the string,
And hurls his bolts afar.

Convictions pierce the stoutest hearts,
They smart, they bleed, they die;
Slain by Immanuel's well-aimed darts,
In helpless heaps they lie.

Behold, he bares his two-edged sword,
And deals almighty blows;
His all-revealing, killing Word
'Twixt joints and marrow goes.

Who can resist him in the fight?
He cuts through coats of mail.
Before the terror of his might
The hearts of rebels fail.

Anon, arrayed in robes of grace,
He rides the trampled plain,
With pity beaming in his face,
And mercy in his train.

---

† *S&T* 1885:169. See also *Autobiography* 4:224 and *SOOH* 4.

Mighty to save he now appears,
Mighty to raise the dead,
Mighty to staunch the bleeding wound,
And lift the fallen head.

Victor alike in love and arms,
Myriads around him bend;
Each captive owns his matchless charms,
Each foe becomes his friend.

They crown him on the battle-field,
They press to kiss his feet;
Their hands, their hearts, their all they yield:
His conquest is complete.

None love him more than those he slew;
His love their hate has slain;
Henceforth their souls are all on fire
To spread his gentle reign.

For further reflection: Hebrews 4:12–13

"I Will Make the Dry Land Springs of Water": The Drop Which Grew into a Torrent. A Personal Experience.[†]

Sung at The Pastors' College Conference 1890

All my soul was dry and dead
Till I learned that Jesus bled;
Bled and suffer'd in my place,
Bearing sin in matchless grace.

Then a drop of heavenly love
Fell upon me from above,
And by secret, mystic art
Reached the centre of my heart.

Glad the story I recount,
How that drop became a fount,
Bubbled up a living well,
Made my heart begin to swell.

All within my soul was praise,
Praise increasing all my days;
Praise which could not silent be:
Floods were struggling to be free.

[†] *S&T* 1890:188.

More and more the waters grew,
Open wide the flood-gates flew,
Leaping forth in streams of song
Flowed my happy life along.

Lo, a river clear and sweet
Laved my glad, obedient feet!
Soon it rose up to my knees,
And I praised and prayed with ease.

Now my soul in praises swims,
Bathes in songs, and psalms, and hymns;
Plunges down into the deeps,
All her powers in worship steeps.

Hallelujah! O my Lord,
Torrents from my soul are poured!
I am carried clean away,
Praising, praising all the day.

In an ocean of delight,
Praising God with all my might,
Self is drowned. So let it be:
Only Christ remains to me.

FOR FURTHER REFLECTION: ISAIAH 41:17—18

JOSEPH HARRALD[†]

Poor old Spurgeon we must urge on,
Not so Joseph Harrald;
Before the sun he's up, like fun,
Ere the lark has carolled.

When worthy Stead has fired his lead,
Not so Joseph Harrald;
Sparkling wit is in his head,
His puns are double-barreled.

Each other wight is wearied quite,
Not so Joseph Harrald;
On he works from morn to night;
Beats poor Douglas Jerrold.

We appear in seedy gear.
Not so Joseph Harrald;
In his glory he'll appear,
As Templars are appareled.

Wine's good drink, as others think,
Not so Joseph Harrald;
Truest blue, he'll never shrink:
Let his brow be laurelled.

[†] *Autobiography* 4:223.

When late he reads, sleep he needs,
Even Joseph Harrald;
Gapes with mouth, with which he feeds,
With which he never quarreled.

Too familiar we, forget that he,
Is the Reverend Joseph Harrald;
From Geneva he; his theology
Is Calvinized and Farelled.

FOR FURTHER REFLECTION: ECCLESIASTES 4:9–12

Dear Mrs. Bennet[†]

Incessantly kind
For years I find
    Yourself and all your party;
The whole hotel
Has learned to excel
    In kindness thorough & hearty.

To every friend
Who joined to send
    Such a varied mass of reading
I beg to express
My thankfulness
    All compliments exceeding.

Hotel des Anglais
Is surnamed wrongly
    Hotel of angels is better;
Watchful and free
I have them to be
    And here I end my letter.

FOR FURTHER REFLECTION: 1 CORINTHIANS 15:58

[†] Mrs. Bennet was the wife of the doctor who cared for Spurgeon when he convalesced in Menton each winter. Apparently, she was also connected to the hotel where he stayed. This poem has never been published but can be found in the collection of the Spurgeon Library in Kansas City, Missouri.

LORD, I WOULD DWELL WITH THEE (PSALM 15)[†]

Lord, I would dwell with Thee,
On Thy most holy hill;
Oh shed Thy grace abroad in me
To mould me to Thy will.

Thy gate of pearl stands wide
For those who walk upright;
But those who basely turn aside
Thou chasest from Thy sight.

Oh tame my tongue to peace,
And tune my heart to love;
From all reproaches may I cease,
Made harmless as a dove.

The vile, though proudly great,
No flatterer find in me;
I count Thy saints of poor estate
Far nobler company.

Faithful, but meekly kind,
Gentle, yet boldly true,
I would possess the perfect mind
Which in my Lord I view.

But, Lord, these graces all
Thy Spirit's work must be;
To Thee, through Jesu's blood I call,
Create them all in me.

FOR FURTHER REFLECTION: PSALM 15:1

[†] *OOH* 15.

THY STRENGTH, O LORD, MAKES GLAD OUR KING (PSALM 21)†

Thy strength, O Lord, makes glad our King
Who once in weakness bow'd the head,
Salvation makes his heart to sing,
For Thou hast raised Him from the dead.

Thou hast bestow'd His heart's desires,
Shower'd on His path Thy blessings down;
His royal pomp all heaven admires;
Thou on His head hast set the crown.

A life eternal as Thy years,
A glory infinite like Thine,
Repays Him for His groans and tears,
And fills His soul with joy divine.

O King, beloved of our souls,
Thine own right hand shall find Thy foes;
Swift o'er their necks Thy chariot rolls,
And earth Thy dreadful vengeance knows.

As glowing oven is Thy wrath,
As flame by furious blast upblown;
With equal heat Thy love breaks forth,
Like wall of fire around Thine own.

Be Thou exalted, King of kings;
In Thine own strength sit Thou on high,
Thy church Thy triumph loudly sings
And lauds Thy glorious majesty.

FOR FURTHER REFLECTION: PSALM 21:6—7

---

† *OOH* 21.

I Will Exalt Thee, Lord of Hosts (Psalm 30)[†]

I will exalt thee, Lord of hosts,
For Thou'st exalted me;
Since Thou hast silenced Satan's boasts
I'll therefore boast in Thee.

My sins had brought me near the grave,
The grave of black despair;
I look'd, but there was none to save
Till I looked up in prayer.

In answer to my piteous cries,
From hell's dark brink I'm brought:
My Jesus saw me from the skies,
And swift salvation wrought.

All through the night I wept full sore,
But morning brought relief;
That hand, which broke my bones before,
Then broke my bonds of grief.

My mourning he to dancing turns,
For sackcloth joy he gives,
A moment, Lord, thine anger burns,
But long Thy favour lives.

Sing with me then, ye favoured men,
Who long have known His grace;
With thanks recall the seasons when
Ye also sought His face.

For further reflection: Psalm 30:4—5

[†] *OOH* 30. Cf. *TD*, 2:53

255

BEHOLD, O LORD, MY DAYS ARE MADE (PSALM 39)[†]

Behold, O Lord, my days are made
A handbreadth at the most;
Ere yet 'tis noon my flower must fade,
And I give up the ghost.

Then teach me, Lord, to know mine end,
And know that I am frail;
To heaven let all my thoughts ascend,
And let not earth prevail.

What is there here that I should wait,
My hope's in Thee alone;
When wilt Thou open glory's gate
And call me to Thy throne?

A stranger in this land am I,
A sojourner with Thee;
Oh be not silent at my cry,
But show Thyself to me.

Though I'm exiled from glory's land,
Yet not from glory's King;
My God is ever near at hand,
And therefore I will sing.

FOR FURTHER REFLECTION: PSALM 39:4—6

[†] *OOH* 39; *S&T* 1892:136, 207.

JESUS, POOREST OF THE POOR (PSALM 41)[†]

Jesus, poorest of the poor!
Man of sorrows! Child of grief!
Happy they whose bounteous store
Minister'd to Thy relief.

Jesus, though Thy head is crown'd,
Crown'd with loftiest majesty,
In Thy members Thou art found,
Plunged in deepest poverty.

Happy they who wash Thy feet,
Visit Thee in Thy distress!
Honour great, and labour sweet,
For Thy sake the saints to bless!

They who feed Thy sick and faint
For Thyself a banquet find;
They who clothe the naked saint
Round *Thy* loins the raiment bind.

Thou wilt keep their soul alive;
From their foes protect their head;
Languishing their strength revive,
And in sickness make their bed

Thou wilt deeds of love repay;
Grace shall gen'rous hearts reward
Here on earth, and in the day
When they meet their reigning Lord.

FOR FURTHER REFLECTION: PSALM 41:1—2

[†] *OOH* 41.

OUR EARS HAVE HEARD, O GLORIOUS GOD (PSALM 44)[†]

Our ears have heard, O glorious God,
What work Thou did'st of old;
And how the heathen felt Thy rod
Our fathers oft have told.

'Twas not Thy people's arm or sword,
But only Thy right hand,
Which scatter'd all the race abhor'd,
And gave Thy tribes their land.

Thou hadst a favour to the seed
Which sprang of Jacob's line,
And still on men afore decreed
Doth love electing shine.

These shall the heritage obtain,
And drive out every sin;
E'en death and hell shall rage in vain,
They *must* the conquest win.

From grace alone their strength shall spring,
Nor bow nor sword can save;
To God alone their Lord and King,
Shall all their banners wave.

[†] *OOH 44.*

Awake, O Lord of Thine elect,
Achieve Thy great design;
Thy saints from Thee alone expect
Salvation's light to shine.

In Thee alone we make our boasts,
And glory all day long,
Arise at once, Thou Lord of hosts,
And fill our mouth with song.

<small>FOR FURTHER REFLECTION: PSALM 44:1–2</small>

THE FOES OF ZION QUAKE
FOR FRIGHT (PSALM 53)[†]

The foes of Zion quake for fright,
Where no fear was they quail;
For well they know that sword of might
Which cuts through coats of mail.

The Lord of old defiled their shields,
And all their spears He scorn'd;
Their bones lay scatter'd o'er the fields,
Unburied and unmourn'd.

Let Zion's foes be fill'd with shame;
Her sons are bless'd of God;
Though scoffers now despise their name,
The Lord shall break the rod.

Oh would our God to Zion turn,
God with salvation clad;
Then Judah's harps should music learn,
And Israel be glad.

FOR FURTHER REFLECTION: PSALM 53:2–3

[†] *OOH* 53. See also *TD* 3:3.

LORD, MAKE MY CONVERSATION CHASTE (PSALM 58)[†]

Lord, make my conversation chaste,
And all my understanding purge,
Lest with the wicked throng I haste,
And down to hell my pathway urge.

They from the womb are all estranged,
The serpent's poison fills each vein,
They're not by wise persuasion changed,
But like the adder deaf remain.

As lions' teeth the hunters break;
As angry torrents soon are dry;
So shall Thy bow swift vengeance take
Upon the proud who truth defy.

As melts the snail with slimy trail;
As thorns consume in rapid blaze;
Before Thy wrath Thy foes shall fail,
Thy whirlwinds shall their souls amaze.

O God, Thou judgest all the earth,
Thy justice cheers my cleansed heart;
Restrain my soul from sinners' mirth,
Lest in their doom I bear a part.

FOR FURTHER REFLECTION: PSALM 58:10–11

[†] *OOH* 58.

O God, Thou Hast Cast Off Thy Saints (Psalm 60)[†]

O God, Thou hast cast off Thy saints;
Thy face Thou dost in anger hide,
And lo, Thy church for terror faints,
While breaches all her walls divide!

Hard things Thou hast upon us laid,
And made us drink most bitter wine,
But still Thy banner we've display'd,
And borne aloft Thy truth divine.

Our courage fails not, though the night
No earthly lamp avails to break,
For Thou wilt soon arise in might,
And of our captors captives make.

Thy right hand shall Thy people aid;
Thy faithful promise makes us strong;
We will Philistia's land invade,
And over Edom chant the song.

In Jesu's name we'll Shechem seize,
And swift divide all Succoth's vale;
E'en Moab's sons shall bow their knees
And Jesu's conquering sceptre hail.

Through Thee we shall most valiant prove,
And tread the foe beneath our feet;
Through Thee our faith shall hills remove,
And small as chaff the mountains beat.

FOR FURTHER REFLECTION: PSALM 60:1–3

[†] *OOH* 60. See also *TD* 3:92.

The Kings of Earth Are in the Hands (Psalm 82)[†]

The kings of earth are in the hands
Of God who reigns on high;
He in their council chamber stands,
And sees with watchful eye.

Though foolish princes tyrants prove,
And tread the godly down;
Though earth's foundations all remove,
He weareth still the crown.

They proudly boast a godlike birth,
In death like men they fall;
Arise, O God, and judge the earth,
And rule the nations all.

When shall Thy Son, the Prince of Peace,
Descend with glorious power?
Then only shall oppression cease:
Oh, haste the welcome hour.

FOR FURTHER REFLECTION: PSALM 82:1–2

[†] *OOH* 82.

O God, Be Thou No Longer Still (Psalm 83)†

O God, be Thou no longer still,
Thy foes are leagued against Thy law;
Make bare Thine arm on Zion's hill,
Great Captain of our Holy War.

As Amalek and Ishmael
Had war forever with Thy seed,
So all the hosts of Rome and hell
Against Thy Son their armies lead.

Though they're agreed in nought beside,
Against Thy truth they all unite;
They rave against the Crucified,
And hate the gospel's growing might,

By Kishon's brook all Jabin's band,
At Thy rebuke were swept away;
O Lord, display Thy mighty hand,
A single stroke shall win the day.

Come, rushing wind, the stubble chase!
Come, sacred fire, the forests burn!
Come, Lord, with all Thy conquering grace,
Rebellious hearts to Jesus turn!

That men may know at once that Thou,
Jehovah, lovest truth right well;
And that Thy church shall never bow
Before the boastful gates of hell.

FOR FURTHER REFLECTION: PSALM 83:1–3

---

† *OOH* 83. See also *TD* 4:52.

Praise the Lord with Exultation (Psalm 111)[†]

Praise the Lord; with exultation
My whole heart my Lord shall praise;
'Midst the upright congregation,
Loftiest hallelujahs raise.

All His works are great and glorious,
Saints review them with delight;
His redemption all victorious
We remember day and night.

Meat He gives to those who fear Him,
Of His covenant mindful still;
Wise are those who much revere Him,
And rejoice to do His will.

For His grace stands fast forever,
His decrees the saints secure;
From His oath He turneth never,
Every promise standeth sure.

Therefore be His praise unceasing,
Be His name forever blest;
And with confidence increasing,
Let us on His promise rest.

For further reflection: Psalm 111:1—3

[†] *OOH* 111.

Blessed Is the Man That Feareth (Psalm 112)[†]

Blessed is the man that feareth,
And delighteth in the Lord,
Wealth, the wealth which truly cheereth,
God shall give Him for reward;
And his children,
Shall be blest around his board.

He shall not be moved for ever,
Though with evil tidings tried;
Nought from God his faith shall sever,
Fix'd his heart shall still abide;
For believers
Are secured on every side.

To the upright light arises,
Darkness soon gives place to day;
While the man who truth despises,
And refuses to obey,
In a moment,
Cursed of God, shall melt away.

Therefore let us praise Jehovah,
Sound His glorious name on high,
Sing His praises, and moreover
By our actions magnify
Our Redeemer,
Who by blood has brought us nigh.

FOR FURTHER REFLECTION: PSALM 112:5—7

---

† *OOH* 112.

Woe's Me That I in Mesech Am (Psalm 120)[†]

Woe's me that I in Mesech am
A sojourner so long;
That I in tabernacles dwell
To Kedar that belong.

My soul with him that hateth peace
Hath long a dweller been;
I am for peace; but when I speak,
For battle they are keen.

My soul distracted mourns and pines
To reach that peaceful shore,
Where all the weary are at rest,
And troublers vex no more.

Fierce burning coals of juniper,
And arrows of the strong,
Await those false and cruel tongues
Which do the righteous wrong.

But as for me my song shall rise
Before Jehovah's throne,
For He has seen my deep distress,
And hearken'd to my groan.

FOR FURTHER REFLECTION: PSALM 120:5—7

---

† *OOH* 120. The first and second verses are a traditional Scotch hymn. Spurgeon composed the third, fourth, and fifth verses. See also *TD* 6:406.

The Holy Ghost Is Here[†]

The Holy Ghost is here,
Where saints in prayer agree,
As Jesu's parting gift He's near
Each pleading company.

Not far away is He,
To be by prayer brought nigh,
But here in present majesty,
As in His courts on high.

He dwells within our soul,
An ever welcome Guest;
He reigns with absolute control,
As Monarch in the breast.

Our bodies are His shrine,
And He th' indwelling Lord;
All hail, thou Comforter divine,
Be evermore adored.

Obedient to Thy will,
We wait to feel Thy power,
O Lord of life, our hopes fulfil,
And bless this hallow'd hour!

FOR FURTHER REFLECTION: 1 CORINTHIANS 6:19–20

[†] *OOH* 451.

WHY SHOULD I SORROW MORE?[†]

Confidence in the Promises

Why should I sorrow more?
I trust a Saviour slain,
And safe beneath His shelt'ring cross,
Unmoved I shall remain.

Let Satan and the world,
Now rage, or now allure;
The promises in Christ are made
Immutable and sure.

The oath infallible
Is now my spirit's trust;
I know that He who spake the word
Is faithful, true, and just.

He'll bring me on my way
Unto my journey's end;
He'll be my Father and my God,
My Saviour and my Friend.

So all my doubts and fears
Shall wholly flee away,
And every mournful night of tears
Be turn'd to joyous day.

All that remains for me
Is but to love and sing,
And wait until the angels come
To bear me to the King.

FOR FURTHER REFLECTION: 2 CORINTHIANS 1:19—20

[†] *OOH* 632. Spurgeon composed the first, fifth, and sixth verses. William
Williams (1717–91) composed the second, third, and fourth verses in 1772.

LORD, THY CHURCH, WITHOUT A PASTOR[†]

Choosing a Minister

Lord, Thy church, without a pastor,
Cries to Thee in her distress;
Hear us, gracious Lord and Master.
And with heavenly guidance bless.

Walking midst Thy lamps all golden,
Thou preservest still the light;
Stars in Thy right hand are holden,
Stars to cheer Thy church's night.

Find us, Lord, the man appointed
Pastor of this flock to be,
One with holy oil anointed,
Meet for us, and dear to Thee.

Send a man, O King of Zion,
Made according to Thine heart,
Meek as lamb, and bold as lion,
Wise to act a shepherd's part.

Grant us now Thy heavenly leading,
Over every heart preside,
Now in answer to our pleading,
All our consultations guide.

FOR FURTHER REFLECTION: ACTS 20:28—29

[†] *OOH* 897.

Risen Lord, Thou Hast Received[†]

Deacons or Elders

Risen Lord, Thou hast received
Gifts to bless the sons of men,
That with souls who have believed,
God might dwell on earth again.

Now these gifts be pleased to send us,
Elders, deacons still supply,
Men whom Thou art pleased to lend us,
All the saints to edify.

Guide us while we here select them,
Let the Holy Ghost be nigh,
Do Thou, Lord, Thyself elect them,
And ordain them from on high.

[*Pause while the election is made.*]

Lord, Thy church invokes Thy blessing
On her chosen {elders'/deacons'} head,
Here we stand our need confessing,
Waiting till Thy grace be shed.

Pour on them Thy rich anointing,
Fill Thy servants with Thy power,
Prove them of Thine own appointing,
Bless them from this very hour.

FOR FURTHER REFLECTION: EPHESIANS 4:11–13

[†] *OOH* 904.

COME, YE WHO BOW TO SOVEREIGN GRACE[†]

Praise to Jesus buried and risen

Come, ye who bow to sovereign grace,
Record Immanuel's love;
Join in a song of noble praise,
To Him who reigns above.

Once in the gloomy grave He lay,
But, by His rising power,
He bore the gates of death away;
Hail! mighty Conqueror.

Here we declare in emblem plain,
Our burial in His grave;
And since in Him we rose again,
We rise from out the wave.

No trust in water do we place,
'Tis but an outward sign;
The great reality is grace,
The fountain, blood divine.

FOR FURTHER REFLECTION: ROMANS 6:3—5

[†] *OOH* 923. Spurgeon composed the third verse. Maria de Fleury (d. 1794) composed the first, second, and fourth verses in 1793.

HERE, O YE FAITHFUL, SEE[†]

Death, Burial, and Resurrection

Here, O ye faithful, see,
Your Lord baptized in woe,
Immersed in seas of agony,
Which all His soul o'erflow.

Here we behold the grave
Which held our buried Head;
We claim a burial in the wave
Because with Jesus dead.

Here, too, we see Him rise,
And live no more to die;
And one with Him by sacred ties
We rise to live on high.

FOR FURTHER REFLECTION: COLOSSIANS 2:11–12

[†] *OOH 934.*

AMIDST US OUR BELOVED STANDS[†]

Jesu's Presence delightful

Amidst us our Beloved stands,
And bids us view His pierced hands;
Points to His wounded feet and side,
Blest emblems of the Crucified.

What food luxurious loads the board,
When at His table sits the Lord!
The wine how rich, the bread how sweet,
When Jesus deigns the guests to meet!

If now, with eyes defiled and dim,
We see the signs, but see not Him,
O may His love the scales displace,
And bid us see Him face to face!

Our former transports we recount,
When with Him in the holy mount,
These cause our souls to thirst anew,
His marr'd but lovely face to view.

Thou glorious Bridegroom of our hearts,
Thy present smile a heaven imparts;
Oh lift the veil, if veil there be,
Let every saint Thy beauties see.

FOR FURTHER REFLECTION: 1 CORINTHIANS 11:27—29

[†] *OOH* 939.

SWEETLY THE HOLY HYMN†

Early Morning Prayer Meeting

Sweetly the holy hymn
Breaks on the morning air;
Before the world with smoke is dim
We meet to offer prayer.

While flowers are wet with dews,
Dew of our souls descend;
Ere yet the sun the day renews;
O Lord, Thy Spirit send.

Upon the battlefield
Before the fight begins,
We seek, O Lord, Thy sheltering shield,
To guard us from our sins.

Ere yet our vessel sails
Upon the stream of day,
We plead, O Lord, for heavenly gales
To speed us on our way.

On the lone mountain side,
Before the morning's light,
The Man of Sorrows wept and cried,
And rose refresh'd with might.

Oh hear *us* then, for we
Are very weak and frail,
We make the Saviour's name our plea,
And surely must prevail.

FOR FURTHER REFLECTION: MARK 1:35–38

---

† *OOH* 974. Cf. *TD* 4:134.

GREAT KING OF ZION NOW[†]

Opening a Place of Worship

Great King of Zion now,
Display Thy matchless grace;
In love the heavens bow
With glory fill this place;
Beneath this roof, oh deign to show
How God can dwell with men below!

Here may Thine ears attend
Our interceding cries,
And grateful praise ascend
All fragrant to the skies;
Here may Thy word melodious sound,
And spread celestial joys around.

Here may th' attentive throng
Imbibe Thy truth and love,
And converts join the song
Of seraphim above;
And willing crowds surround Thy board,
With sacred joy and sweet accord.

Here may our unborn sons
And daughters sound Thy praise,
And shine, like polish'd stones,
Through long succeeding days;
Here, Lord, display Thy saving power,
Until the last triumphant hour.

FOR FURTHER REFLECTION: ISAIAH 66:1–2

[†] *OOH* 1020. Spurgeon composed the third and fourth verses. Benjamin Francis (1734–99) composed the first and second verses in 1787.

OUR FATHER, BLESS THE BOUNTEOUS STORE[†]

Before Meat

Our Father, bless the bounteous store
Wherewith Thou hast our table spread,
With grateful songs we all adore,
And bless the hand by which we're fed.

HEAVENLY FATHER, GRANT THY BLESSING[‡]

Before Meat

Heavenly Father, grant Thy blessing
On the food before us spread,
All our tongues are now confessing,
By Thy hand alone we're fed,
And Thou givest,
Best of all, the living bread.

FOR FURTHER REFLECTION: JAMES 1:16—18

[†] *OOH* 1055.
[‡] *OOH* 1056.

Join to Bless the Bounteous Giver[†]

After Meat

Join to bless the bounteous Giver,
For the food He here bestows;
From His goodness like a river
Every earthly blessing flows.

We Thank Thee, Father, for the Love[‡]

After Meat

We thank Thee, Father, for the love
Which feeds us here below.
And hope in fairer realms above,
Celestial feasts to know.

FOR FURTHER REFLECTION: MATTHEW 6:31–33

[†] *OOH* 1058.
[‡] *OOH* 1059.

At Midnight Praise the Lord[†]

Songs in the Night

At midnight praise the Lord,
Ye who this [His] temple throng;
Lift up your hearts with one accord,
And close the year with song.

Light up the altar fire,
Forget the chilly night;
Let grateful love all hearts inspire,
Praise God with all your might.

Into the coming year,
March ye with banners high;
Nought in the future need ye fear,
For Israel's God is nigh.

But march with voice of praise,
Let music lead your way;
To God the Lord your voices raise,
On this the [glad] New Year's Day.

FOR FURTHER REFLECTION: JAMES 5:7–8

[†] *SOOH 64.*

CROWN HIM LORD OF ALL[†]

A new adaptation and arrangement of Perronet's hymn; 1870

TO BE SUNG BY ALL BELIEVERS —
All hail the power of Jesus' name!
Let angels prostrate fall;
Bring forth the royal diadem,
And crown him Lord of all.

We who compose his court below,
And wait his gracious call,
In marshall'd ranks before him bow,
And crown him Lord of all.

MEN'S VOICES —
Let men and sires loud praises bring
To him who drank the gall;
Adore their now ascended King,
And crown him Lord of all.

Lo, in our strength and vigor we
Would crowd his royal hall,
Bring forth our sweetest minstrelsy,
And crown him Lord of all.

[†] *SOOH* 18. The first verse was written by Edward Perronet (1721–92). The rest was composed by Spurgeon. "The following hymn has been sung at the Tabernacle with remarkable effect. We print it in the *Sword and Trowel* because we hope that other congregations will be glad to use it. They can have it of our publishers for sixpence per hundred. Of course the eighth verse can only be sung where there are orphans, but all the rest, if only the voices mentioned are allowed to join in their appointed verses, will go very sweetly, and make up a charming variety of praise unto the Most High." *S&T* 1877:180.

WOMEN'S VOICES —
Now to the Lord, of woman born,
Who slept in Bethlehem's stall,
Matrons and maids lift up their song,
And crown him Lord of all.

For unto us a Son is given,
To save from sin and thrall;
We join the angelic choirs of heaven,
And crown him Lord of all.

CHILDREN AND THE ORPHANS —
Because he suffers babes to sing,
And smiles on children small,
We make our loud hosannas ring,
And crown him Lord of all.

We who had else been fatherless,
Our Jesus "Father" call;
and by his care his name we bless,
And crown him Lord of all.

TO BE SUNG BY ALL —
Now in one glad exulting song
We at his footstool fall,
Unite with all the blood-washed throng,
And crown him Lord of all.

FOR FURTHER REFLECTION: REVELATION 19:11—13

Fly to Jesus[†]

Guilty sinner, fly to Jesus;
He alone can purge our guilt;
From each deadly sin He frees us,
'Twas for this His blood was spilt.
Come, and welcome;
Come this moment, if thou wilt.

Empty sinner, haste to Jesus,
For in Him all fulness dwells,
And His inmost soul it pleases
When a longing soul He fills
Be not backward;
He invites whoever wills.

Hopeless sinner, look to Jesus,
In His death thy ransom see,
From despair His word releases,
Trust in Him, and fear shall flee
High as heaven
Are his thoughts of love to thee.

Worst of sinners, come to Jesus,
He has said He'll cast out none,
Come with all thy foul diseases,
He can cure them every one;
And, with wonder,
Thou shalt sing what grace has done.

FOR FURTHER REFLECTION: COLOSSIANS 1:19–20

[†] Robert Shindler, *From the Usher's Desk to the Tabernacle Pulpit: The Life and Labors of Charles Haddon Spurgeon* (New York: A. C. Armstrong and Son, 1892), 262.

WHEN BROKEN, TUNELESS, STILL, O LORD[†]

July 1889

When broken, tuneless, still, O Lord,
This voice shall yet *Thy blood* record,
Its virtue tried so long;

Till, sinking low with calm decay,
Its feeble accents melt away
Into a seraph's song;

And then along the eternal tide
I'll chant the praise of Him who died
To all the blood-washed throng.

FOR FURTHER REFLECTION: JUDE 24—25

[†] James Douglas, *The Prince of Preachers: A Sketch; a Portraiture; and a Tribute* (London: Morgan and Scott, 1892), 121. "The following lines, written in an album of a friend, and signed C. H. SPURGEON, July, 1889, may be cited as showing how his soul was swayed by the truth in question." The first two verses are modified from Robert Grant's (1779–1838) hymn, "Thy Mercy Heard My Infant Prayer." The third stanza appears original to Spurgeon.

ACKNOWLEDGMENTS

William Cowper once wrote of the mysterious way in which God moves. While working on this project, I had plenty of time to reflect on the mysterious and gracious providence of God that I should have the privilege of transcribing these poems and making them available. I'm grateful for the trustees at Midwestern Baptist Theological Seminary for purchasing the Spurgeon collection and for continuing to invest in the work of the Spurgeon Library. I'm grateful for our president, Jason Allen, for his vision for the Spurgeon Library and leadership of the seminary. Jason Duesing, the provost, has also been an ongoing encouragement to our work. I'm also thankful for Madison Trammel, Michael McEwen, and the rest of the team at B&H Academic for their interest in this project and their expertise in bringing it to life.

I'm thankful for the team of young scholars and researchers that I get to work with in the Spurgeon Library. This includes Jaron Button, John Crawford, Ethan Collins, Micah Powell, Joshua Redd, David Aust, and Elijah Walls, who helped proofread my transcriptions. Thanks also to Joshua Redd for his work on the photos. I'm also thankful to Aaron Day, who compiled the citations and assisted with research for this project. Additionally, I'm grateful for Spurgeon scholars around the world who have been a source of feedback and support for me in this project, including Matt Boswell, Tom Breimaier, Alex DiPrima, and Ray Rhodes Jr.

As always, I am thankful to my children, who found this project more interesting than others in the past. Most of all, I'm thankful for my dear wife, whose support makes my work in Spurgeon scholarship possible. She has been a faithful and loving companion to me on this pilgrim journey, a reminder of God's undeserved grace in my life.

In writing these poems, Spurgeon's eyes were fixed on the triune God, and in reading these poems, may we also grow in our hope in Him.

INDEX